Dear Family Member,

Sight words are those frequently-used, non-decodable words that  reading fluency. Ask any teacher or educational expert what's the onl to master these sight words and they'll all agree—practice!

We've created the *Scholastic 100 Words* workbook series to give y tice. Working with literacy specialists and classroom teachers, we identified the 100 words your child needs to know by third grade. Then we developed inviting educational activities to give your child opportunities to read, write, and use these words.

The sight words in *Scholastic's 100 Words Kids Need to Read by 3rd Grade* are divided into seven word groups. The words in each group are introduced in context and reinforced throughout the activities. As your child moves through this workbook, he or she will move from visual recognition of sight words to genuine mastery. Your child will also gain important preparatory experience that will later help with standardized tests.

To reinforce the message that skill-building helps make reading fluent—*and fun*— we've included a wonderful "mini-book" at the end of each word group section. This mini-book weaves all the words from the word group into a lively story your child will love reading aloud. And to encourage your child's love of reading, we've also included a list of 100 Great Books to Read by 3rd Grade.

The journey through these workbook pages will help young readers make the successful transition from learning to read to reading to learn. Enjoy the trip!

David Goddy
Publisher, Scholastic Magazines

Tips For Family Members

Join in with your child on the activity pages:
- ✓ Read the directions aloud.
- ✓ Help your child get started by making sure he or she knows what to do.
- ✓ Point out examples, such as circles or underlines, in the directions. Show your child how to use the illustrations or photos to provide clues for words.

Share the mini-books with your child:

- ✓ To assemble a mini-book, detach the two pages where perforated. Fold first sheet at dotted line so that pages 1 and 8 of mini-book are on the outside, and pages 2 and 7 are on the inside. Fold second sheet so that pages 3 and 6 are on the outside, and pages 4 and 5 are on the inside. Insert second folded sheet into first folded sheet. The mini-book cover will be on the outside and story pages will follow in number order.

- ✓ Ask your child to read the story aloud to you. Using the word list on page 3, ask your child to find all the words from the word group in the mini-book.

Read, read, read!

- ✓ Visit your library or bookstore and help your child find the 100 great 3rd grade books listed on our poster.

Table of Contents

Editorial Consultant: Mary C. Rose, Orange County Public Schools, Orlando, Florida **Writers:** Anne Schreiber, Gail Tuchman, Kathryn McKeon **Illustrators:** Greg Paprocki, Valeria Petrone, Jackie Snider **Art Director:** Nancy Sabato **Composition:** Kevin Callahan, BNGO Books **Cover:** Red Herring Design

PHOTO CREDITS CORBIS: Dave G. Houser: 191; **Kelly-Mooney Photography:** 22 (marbles); **Royalty-Free:** 25 (bell, street light, knight), 92, 167, 196 (lemons, limes, exit sign), 237 (necklaces); **Tria Giovan:** 237 (hats). GETTY IMAGES: PhotoDisc: 22 (cookies), 90 (car), 105 (bus), 172; **The Image Bank:** 25 (shell), 196 (cars). PHOTO EDIT (Long Beach, CA): A. Ramey: 149; **Amy Etra:** 25 (well), 173, 233; **Barbara Stitzer:** 170; **Cindy Charles:** 47 (boy eats pizza); **David Young-Wolff:** 5 (kids running), 22 & 60 (bicycle), 42 (girl drawing), 47 (boy eats cereal), 49 (grandfather), 156, 237 (ice cream cones); **Davis Barker:** 153; **Deborah Davis:** 90 (ferry); **Dennis MacDonald:** 77, 86; **Elena Rooraid:** 12; **Erich Lessing:** 171 (jug); **Felicia Martinez:** 60 (toy car), 90 (hoe), 237 (red and white coat); **Jonathan Nourok:** 105 (base), 161 (candy); **Mary Steinbacher:** 5 (swan); **Michael Newman:** 119 & 140 & 165 (boy detectives), 226, 237 (three color coat); **Myrleen Ferguson Cate:** 49 (boy), 52 (boy and dog), 90 (sun), 192; **Novastock:** 101, 189; **Pam Rogow:** 230; **Richard Hutchings:** 47 (girl with mirror); **Robert Brenner:** 137, 171 (dig site); **Rudi Von Briel:** 78, 168, 212; **Spencer Grand:** 25 (flower); **Susan Van Etten:** 127, 232; **Tom Carter:** 209; **Tony Freeman:** 5 (saw), 22 & 161 (pamphlets), 81 (tree, beetle), 90 (shoes), 223 (target); **Will Hart:** 47 (boy in bed). PHOTO RESEARCHERS (New York, NY): Alan & Linda Detrick: 109–112 (silhouetted cicadas) 109R, 110C; **Bill Bachman:** 52 (girls playing); **Danny Brass:** 111L, 112L; **Gary Meszaros:** 109L; **J. H. Robinson:** 111R; **Jeff Greenberg:** 105 (taxi driver); **Jerry Wachter:** 103 & 196; **Jim Selby/Science Photo Library:** 42 (boy with cast); **Ken M. Highfill:** 110L; **Millard H. Sharp:** 122; **Rafael Macia:** 89; **Steve Maslowski:** 106; **Tom McHugh:** 81 (mouse); **Wayne Lawler:** 114; **Will & Deni McIntyre:** 105 (playing cards). SODA (Scholastic Online Digital Archive): Artville via SODA: 70 & 141; **David Lawrence:** 161 (popcorn); **Digital Stock via SODA:** 42 (woman with notebook); **Digital Vision via SODA:** 25 (boy with kite), 183; **Dynamic Graphics:** 94; **Francis Clark Westfield:** 52 (girl painting); **Gerri Hernandez:** 196 (boy waving); **John Lei:** 161 (airplane); **Ken Karp:** 47 (boy with backpack); **Photodisc via SODA:** 8, 25 (snowy landscape, foot), 42 (father & daughter, woman on phone, clown), 55, 81 (bird, butterfly), 85, 105 (bee), 134, 196 (boy fishing), 222, 240; **Richard Lee:** 120; **Stanley Bach:** 64. SUPERSTOCK (Jacksonville, FL): 6, 26, 47 (food), 60 and 90 (pie), 80, 81 (roots, bear), 84, 95, 110R, 112R, 237 (dogs).

My 100 Words

Group 1

answer	know	told
believe	should	would
could	tell	write
enough	these	wrote
knew	those	

Group 2

bought	drew	talk
bring	held	think
brought	hold	thought
buy	hurt	walk
draw	laugh	

Group 3

above	does	going
around	done	grew
because	far	grow
behind	flew	through
below	fly	very

Group 4

always	light	once
it's	may	right
its	month	start
just	must	wrong
left	never	year

Group 5

away	kind	round
call	much	shall
find	only	too
found	pull	upon
full	put	

Group 6

about	live	though
again	middle	warm
carry	own	which
city	ready	word
clean	sure	

Group 7

beautiful	learn	together
been	neither	tomorrow
different	several	trouble
either	straight	yesterday
frighten	today	

Enough Is Enough

Circle the words that rhyme with **enough**.

(puff)   through   thought   (stuff)

(tough)   (huff)   (rough)   bug

Now finish this sentence using some
of the words you circled.

That wolf was too __Rough__ and __tough__

when he told the pigs, "I'll __huff__, and I'll

__Puff__, and I'll blow your house down."

Many Answers

Finish the sentences below with words you can make using the letters in the word **answer**. The first example is done for you.

1. What costume will you __wear__ to the play?

2. I will cut this wood with a ___Saw___.

3. I ___was___ eating dinner when the phone rang.

4. The beautiful white ___Swan___ glided through the water.

5. My Dad always watches the ___war___ on television.

6. I bought a ___new___ book at the store.

7. My friend and I ___Ran___ in a race.

8. I'd like to eat ___a___ ice cream cone.

Woody the Woodchuck

Use the words from the box to finish the sentences. You can use the same word more than once. Hint: You may need to use capital letters.

Word Box

wood	would	could

Could you please get me a glass of water?

The _wood_ from an oak tree is very strong.

I _Could_ not reach the top shelf.

Bugs like to live in the soft _wood_ of rotting trees.

I _Could_ not ride a bike until this year.

She said she _would_ be able to go to the party.

Now use the words from the word box to finish this riddle.

How much _wood_ _would_ a _wood_ chuck chuck if a _wood_ chuck _Could_ chuck _wood_?

Puzzling Dinner

The picture clues will help you make words.
Write the words on the lines so you can read the letter.
Hint: You may need to use capital letters.

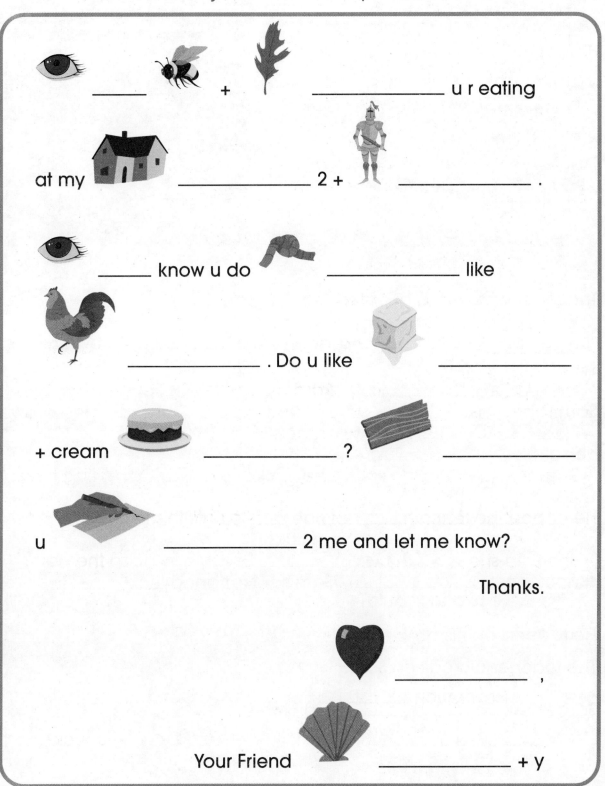

_____ + _____ u r eating

at my _____ 2 + _____ .

_____ know u do _____ like

_____ . Do u like _____

+ cream _____ ? _____

u _____ 2 me and let me know?

Thanks.

_____ ,

Your Friend _____ + y

Right? Write!

Homophones are words that sound the same, but are spelled differently and have different meanings. Circle the word that finishes the sentence and write it on the line.

The teacher asked a question.

"If you _____ the answer, _____ it down," she said.
　　　　(know, no)　　　　　　　　　　　　(right, write)

Sam raised his _____ hand. "I _____ the answer,"
　　　　　　　(right, write)　　　　　　　　　(no, know)
he said.

He hoped the teacher _____ call on him.
　　　　　　　　　　(wood, would)

"Knock on _____ ," Sam said for good luck.
　　　　　(wood, would)

He tapped on his desk.

The teacher did call on Sam.

Sam knew the _____ answer!
　　　　　　(right, write)

A Loony Letter

Before you read the story, fill in the list of words in the box. Then write those words in the story and read your loony letter out loud!

1. _____
   adjective

2. _____
   type of transportation

3. _____
   body of water

4. _____
   animal

5. _____
   color

6. _____
   noun

7. _____
   number

8. _____
   adjective

Dear Mom and Dad,

I have a _____ story to tell you about what happened
          1

to me at camp. Have you ever rowed a _____? Well, we
                                        2

took one out on the _____. In the middle of the water,
                      3

we saw a giant _____. It was _____. It had big
                 4   5

_____ on its head. It had _____ legs. We rowed
 6   7

away as fast as we could!

When we got back, we told everybody about what we saw.

No one believed us. They thought we were _____.
                                           8

I should have stayed on land!

I will write again soon.

Love,

_____
your name

Words That Rock!

Write these words in alphabetical order on the musical notes:
could, knew, write, wrote, answer, know, believe, tell.

2 _____

1 _____

3 _____

4 _____

5 _____

6 _____

7 _____

8 _____

Treasure

Unscramble the 14 letters in the picture to solve the riddle.

What did the boy say when his brother asked him to find a treasure chest?

___ _____ ____ ____

_____

Camp Days

Use the words from the word box to finish the puzzle.

Word Box

enough   should   write   told   could   wrote

Across

1. When I'm in camp, I _____ letters to my friends.

3. I _____ my friends at camp that I would be back to see them next summer.

4. I _____ go swimming tomorrow because I didn't go today.

Down

1. I _____ a letter to my parents telling them all about my boat trip.

2. I ate _____ popcorn at camp to last me all year.

5. I _____ have gone swimming, but I didn't want to.

The Silk Road

Circle the 10 mistakes in this passage.
Write the correct words on the lines below.

The Silk Road was a group of paths that connected China and Europe more than 1,000 years ago. Ancient Chinese people and other traders new about these paths and wood use them for travel. The Chinese people cood carry silk over these roads. That's why the paths were called the Silk Road. The ancient Chinese people know how to make silk before anyone else. They were the only people who new the secret, and they wood not told anyone else. Camels were often used to carry things over the long road. Theeze camels were able to go long distances over dry land. Then one day, thoze paths were not used as much. People started to believed that traveling over water was safer.

_____ _____ _____ _____

_____ _____ _____ _____

_____ _____

Alien Message

An alien you met sent you a secret message from his home planet.
You have to use the code to find out what it says.

Alien Code Manual

d	+		r	©
e	^		t	ō
I	*		u	!
l	å		w	«
o	#		y	&

*   ō # å +   & # !   *   « # ! å +   « © * ō ^

___ _____ ____ __ _____ _____!

Scrambled!

Unscramble the words and write them on the lines.

lveeeib   __ (1) __ __ __ __ __ __

guenho   __ (2) (3) (4) __ __

wasren   (5) (6) __ __ __ __

dulsoh   __ (7) __ __ __ (8)

trowe   __ __ __ (9) __

eshte   __ __ __ __ __

dogo   __ __ __ __

Now unscramble the circled letters to solve this riddle:

How good did the cat think the mouse was?

$\underline{}_{4}$ $\underline{}_{2}$ $\underline{}_{2}$ $\underline{}_{8}$ $\underline{}_{1}$ $\underline{}_{6}$ $\underline{}_{2}$ $\underline{}_{3}$ $\underline{}_{4}$ $\underline{}_{7}$

$\underline{}_{9}$ $\underline{}_{2}$ $\underline{}_{1}$ $\underline{}_{5}$ $\underline{}_{9}$!

What's for Dinner?

Read the story. Circle the letter for the answer that best fits the question.

Will and his mother went out for dinner at the Big Food Cafe. Will's friend had told him that all the food there was really, really big.

Will's mother said if Will ate all his food, he could order dessert. She didn't really believe that Will would finish all the food on his plate. When Will's hamburger came, it was the biggest burger he had ever seen. He knew it would be hard to eat all of it, but he would try.

Will finished his burger. He knew he had eaten enough. But Will really wanted to try a Big Cone, so he ordered it. When the dessert arrived, it was the biggest cone Will had ever seen. He didn't know what to do. The answer came to him.

"Mom," said Will, "want to share?" Will and his mother ate that Big Cone all up!

1. What did Will eat first?
   a. burger
   b. ice cream
   c. salad

2. Why was it hard for Will to finish his food?
   a. He didn't like it.
   b. It was too big.
   c. He had eaten before he came.

3. How did Will solve his problem?
   a. He ate another burger.
   b. He didn't eat the ice cream.
   c. He shared the ice cream with his mother.

4. **Knew** is the past tense of what word?
   a. know
   b. think
   c. thought

5. What does the sentence, **The answer came to him** mean?
   a. Will was taking a test.
   b. Will suddenly thought of the solution to his problem.
   c. Will's mother was asking him a question.

6. Where in the dictionary would the word **believe** go?
   a. between answer and ant
   b. between could and would
   c. between answer and could

More or Less

Use the key to find out what each letter is worth.
Then add or subtract to find out which word is worth **more** (>)
or **less** (<). Hint: Some words are **equal** (=) or worth the same.

Letter and Number Key

a = 1 b = 2 c = 3 d = 4 e = 5 f = 1 g = 2 h = 3 i = 4

j = 5 k = 1 l = 2 m = 3 n = 4 o = 5 p = 1 q = 2 r = 3

s = 4 t = 5 u = 1 v = 2 w = 3 x = 4 y = 5 z = 1

Circle the correct symbol.

Which word is worth more: **tell** or **told**?

t e l l   < = >   t o l d

__ __ __ __ = ____   __ __ __ __ = ____

Which word is worth more: **answer** or **know**?

a n s w e r   < = > k n o w

__ __ __ __ __ __ = ____   __ __ __ __ = ____

What's worth more: something you **wrote** or something you will **write**?

w r o t e   < = > w r i t e

__ __ __ __ __ = ____   __ __ __ __ __ = ____

Which word is worth more: **these** or **those**?

t h e s e   < = > t h o s e

__ __ __ __ __ = ____   __ __ __ __ __ = ____

Use the words from the word box to answer these questions.

Word Box

tell	answer	those	wrote	could
told	these	write	would	enough

Which two words have the same value as **answer**?

a   n   s   w   e   r

__ __ __ __ __ __ = ____

__ __ __ __ __ = ____

__ __ __ __ __ __ __ = ____

If you add **tell** to **told**, you get the same value as if you added **could** and what other word from the word box?

t   e   l   l   +   t   o   l   d

__ __ __ __ + __ __ __ __ = 30

c   o   u   l   d   +

__ __ __ __ __ + __ __ __ __ __ = 30

Find a 2-letter word that equals the difference between the values of **answer** and **tell**.

a   n   s   w   e   r   -   t   e   l   l

__ __ __ __ __ __ - __ __ __ __ = __

__ __ = ____

Mind Your These and Those

Look at the pictures. Then write **these** or **those**, whichever word best finishes the sentence. Hint: You may need to use capital letters.

_____ running shoes are very comfortable.

Look at _____ runners go!

Look at _____ blue trucks in there.

Do you see _____ horses on that hill.

I bought _____ red trucks.

I want to ride _____ horses.

Would you like to eat _____ apple slices for lunch?

Would you like _____ grapes instead?

_____ red birds are far away.

_____ yellow birds are close by.

The Cinderella Test

How much do you know about Cinderella?
Use the words from the word box to finish these sentences.

Word Box

believe   could   knew   know   told   would   wrote

The prince's mother_____ a note inviting the whole town to the ball.

Cinderella's stepsisters _____ her that she _____ not go to the ball.

The prince didn't _____ where to find Cinderella.

Cinderella didn't really _____ the Fairy Godmother when she told her to stop dancing by midnight.

Cinderella _____ she loved the prince the minute she saw him.

The prince _____ not stop looking until he found Cinderella.

Good Enough

Solve each math problem. Then circle the correct answer.

Jo needs 32 cookies for her birthday party.

She made two batches. One batch had 16 cookies.

The other batch had 14 cookies.

Jo has (too few, enough) cookies for her party.

Phillipe had 50 marbles. He lost 17 in his yard.

He went to the store and brought 6 more marbles.

He needs 48 marbles to play his game.

Phillipe has (too few, enough) marbles

to play his game.

Tanya collected 29 baseball cards.

She traded 7 star cards for 15 basic cards.

She needs 35 cards to fill up all the slots

in her baseball card book.

Does Tanya have (too few, enough) cards

to fill her book?

Terry has to bicycle 10 hours to raise money

for his school.

He rode 2 hours one day, 4 hours on the second,

and 4 hours on the final day.

Did Terry ride (too few, enough) miles

to raise the money?

Puppy Love

Move this puppy through his day so he can go to sleep. The right path has words in the present tense (something that is happening now). The wrong path has words in the past tense (something that already happened).

Synonym Bowling

Synonyms are words with similar meanings. Match each word to its synonym by drawing a line between the ball and the correct pin.

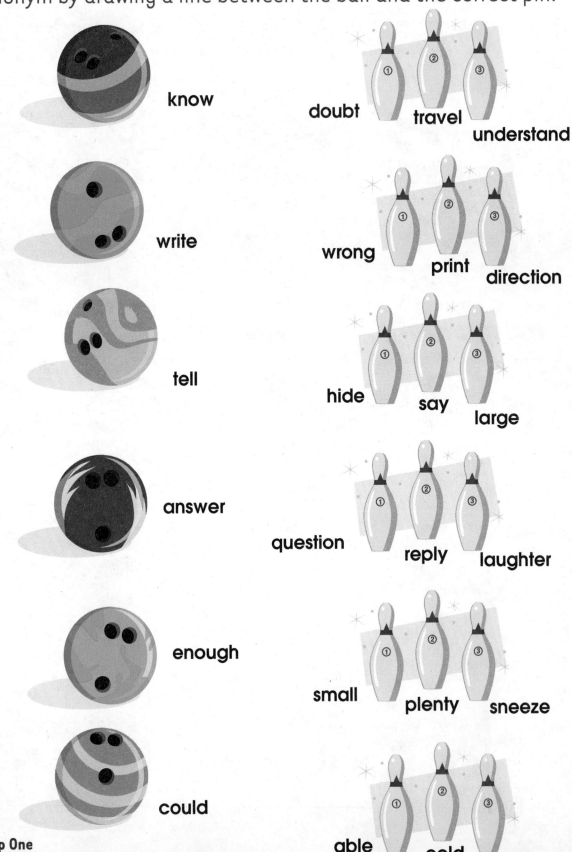

know

doubt ① travel ② understand ③

write

wrong ① print ② direction ③

tell

hide ① say ② large ③

answer

question ① reply ② laughter ③

enough

small ① plenty ② sneeze ③

could

able ① cold ② unable ③

Rhyme Lines

Draw a line between the rhyming words.

bell

bow

kite

tell

well

write

snow

know

light

knight

shell

toe

Pairs of Pears

Circle the pear with the word that is the past tense of the word that is in each box. Then use it to finish the sentence.

 know

knew   known   knowed

You _____ her from your soccer team last year.

tell

tolded   told   telled

I _____ you to bring a jacket.

know

knowd   knewed   knew

I _____ you would remember to bring the peanut butter.

write

written   wrote   writtened

I still have the letter you _____ me last year.

tell

told   tole   telded

I _____ you about the party last week.

Word Search

Find these words in the puzzle below:
**believe, enough, knew, know, these,
those, write, wrote, answer.**

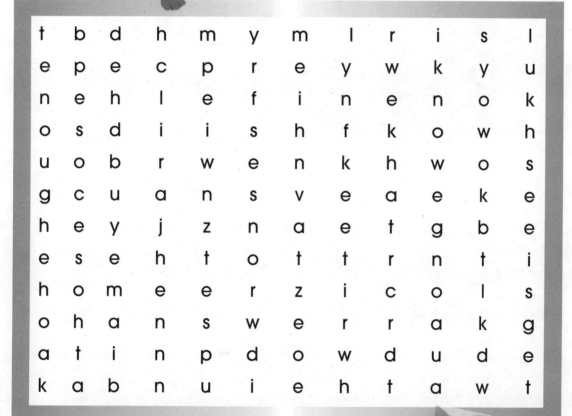

t	b	d	h	m	y	m	l	r	i	s	l
e	p	e	c	p	r	e	y	w	k	y	u
n	e	h	l	e	f	i	n	e	n	o	k
o	s	d	i	i	s	h	f	k	o	w	h
u	o	b	r	w	e	n	k	h	w	o	s
g	c	u	a	n	s	v	e	a	e	k	e
h	e	y	j	z	n	a	e	t	g	b	e
e	s	e	h	t	o	t	t	r	n	t	i
h	o	m	e	e	r	z	i	c	o	l	s
o	h	a	n	s	w	e	r	r	a	k	g
a	t	i	n	p	d	o	w	d	u	d	e
k	a	b	n	u	i	e	h	t	a	w	t

Check!

Fill in the box with a check ✓ for correct sentences and an **X** for incorrect sentences.

1. I forgot to write my report on oceans. ☐

2. My friend write me a postcard from Canada. ☐

3. I wrote the instructions for feeding the fish and

   left them on the table. ☐

4. Did you wrote your mother a note to tell her where we went? ☐

5. He didn't wrote me the whole time he was away. ☐

6. Tell her to write a list of ingredients for the cookies. ☐

7. My teacher wrote the homework on the board. ☐

8. The dentist write down how to brush. ☐

9. Don't forgot to wrote. ☐

10. I wrote you a poem for your birthday. ☐

The Little Plant that Could

Put this cartoon in order by numbering the panels 1-6.
The first one is done for you.

"I think you should look at this. Something strange is happening. The plant is growing very quickly."

"This plant looks dry. Could you please get me a cup of water?"

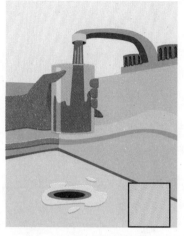

"No, you should not fill the cup all the way up. You should just fill it half way."

"The plant is growing faster than it should. I think we should GET OUT OF HERE!"

"Now I could give the plant a drink."

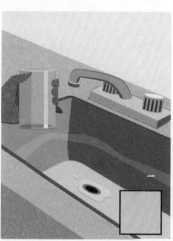

"Yes, I could get you a cup of water. Should I fill it all the way up?"

Silly Questions

Use one phrase from the **Action Box** and one phrase from the **Thing Box** to finish each question. Then draw a picture of your sentence.

Action Box

reach the

bring me the

touch the

Thing Box

bird's beak

giraffe's hat

snail in his shell

Would you _____ _____ ?

Could you _____ _____ ?

Should you _____ _____ ?

Word Bingo Game Boards

Board 1 (top left):

answer	tell	told	knew	believe
wrote	told	know	write	answer
believe	should	Wild Word	write	knew
should	told	tell	know	answer
tell	wrote	believe	told	know

Board 2 (top right):

should	knew	answer	told	write
write	told	know	believe	answer
wrote	should	Wild Word	knew	tell
tell	told	believe	know	answer
know	believe	tell	wrote	knew

Board 3 (bottom left):

believe	wrote	write	know	tell
write	tell	answer	believe	knew
wrote	answer	Wild Word	told	believe
write	told	should	tell	knew
should	knew	told	know	answer

Board 4 (bottom right):

know	wrote	knew	answer	answer
told	should	knew	answer	tell
tell	wrote	Wild Word	write	told
answer	know	write	told	knew
write	tell	believe	know	knew

Word Bingo, see page 35

Word Bingo, see page 35

Word Bingo Clue Cards

What you give after a question.	Starts with the letter t and is a synonym for say.	Rhymes with the opposite of young.	Rhymes with could.	Complete this sentence. I ___ you not to go there.	The root word of unbelievable.
When you add the word not, this word becomes a contraction.	If you scramble this word, it spells tower.	A 2-syllable word with a silent w.	What you do when someone is telling the truth.	This word means to communicate using a pen and paper.	Rhymes with few.
A 2-syllable word starting with the letter a.	The root of the word knowledge.	The opposite of mistrust.	A synonym for understand.	Complete this sentence: ___ a short paragraph about your vacation.	In the dictionary, this word would come after knack and before knit.
Present tense of told.	In the dictionary, this word would come after tall and before ten.	In the dictionary, this word comes after write and before vote.	Present tense of knew.	Opposite of question.	Past tense of write.
A 2 syllable word beginning with the letter b.	Rhymes with something you can ring.	Past tense of tell.	Past tense of a word that that means to understand.	Complete this sentence. I ___ do my homework now.	A homophone of the opposite of left.
Rhymes with the opposite of day.	The opposite of kept a secret.	This word has the same beginning sound as shell.	This word's homophone is the opposite of yes.	Rhymes with the word boat.	This word's homophone is the opposite of old.

Word Bingo, see page 35

Clue Card	Clue Card	Clue Card	Clue Card	Clue Card	Clue Card
Clue Card	Clue Card	Clue Card	Clue Card	Clue Card	Clue Card
Clue Card	Clue Card	Clue Card	Clue Card	Clue Card	Clue Card
Clue Card	Clue Card	Clue Card	Clue Card	Clue Card	Clue Card
Clue Card	Clue Card	Clue Card	Clue Card	Clue Card	Clue Card
Clue Card	Clue Card	Clue Card	Clue Card	Clue Card	Clue Card

Word Bingo, see page 35

Word Bingo Directions

Play this game with
your family or friends.

You'll Need:
- the word bingo game boards
  from page 31
- the clue cards from page 33
- 20 markers (coins, beans, pebbles, paper clips, etc.)

How to Play:
- Shuffle the clue cards and leave them face down.
- Each player takes a game board. It's okay if other players see
  your board.
- Have someone who is not playing read the clue cards out loud.

If a word clue is called that matches a word on your board, cover
that word with a marker. If that word appears on your board more
than once, you may only cover one of the words at a time.

You may place a marker on the Wild Word square in response to
any clue in the game. You can only use the Wild Word square one
time and cannot mark another word in the same turn.

The first player to cover five squares in a row (across, up and
down, or diagonally) wins the game.

If you use up all the clue cards before someone wins, reshuffle the
clue cards and use them again.

Word Group 1 Answer Key

4   circle: stuff; puff; tough; huff; rough; write: rough; tough; huff; puff (order may vary)

5   2. saw; 3. was; 4. swan; 5. news; 6. new; 7. ran; 8. an

6   Would; wood; could; wood; could; would; wood; could; wood; wood; could; wood

7   I believe you are; house; tonight; I know you do not like chicken; you; ice cream cake; Would you write to; know; Love; Shelly

8   know; write; right; know; would; wood; right

9   answers will vary

10   1. answer; 2. believe; 3. could; 4. knew; 5. know; 6. tell; 7. write; 8. wrote

11   I would if I could.

12   **Across:** 1. write; 3. told; 4. should **Down:** 1. wrote; 2. enough; 5. could

13   circle: new; wood; cood; know; new; wood; told; Theeze; thoze; believed; write: knew; would; could; new; knew; would tell; These; those; believe

14   I told you I would write!

15   believe; enough, answer; should; wrote; these; good; good enough to eat!

16   1. a; 2. b; 3. c; 4. a; 5. b; 6. c

18–19   circle: <, >, <, = write: and; enough; would; at = 6

20   These, those; those, these; those, these; these, those; Those; These

21   wrote; told; could; know; believe; knew; would

22   too few; too few; enough; enough

23   see below

24   draw lines to understand; print; say; reply; plenty; able

25   tell = bell, well, shell; write = kite, light, knight; know = snow, bow, toe

26   knew; told; knew; wrote; told

27   see below

28   1. ✓ 2. x; 3. ✓ 4. x; 5. x; 6. ✓ 7. ✓ 8. x; 9. x; 10. ✓

29   left to right: 5; 1; 3; 6; 4; 2

30   answers will vary

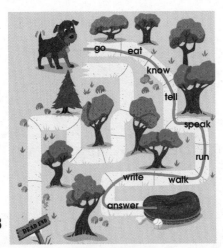

page 23

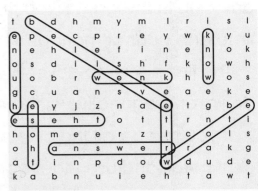

page 27

My cousin from Florida answered me:

"Thank you for your help, M.T.W.B.!"

He sent something else for my friends and me—

a photograph of our manatee!

fold & assemble

M.T.W.B.

Written by Gail Tuchman

Illustrated by Valeria Petrone

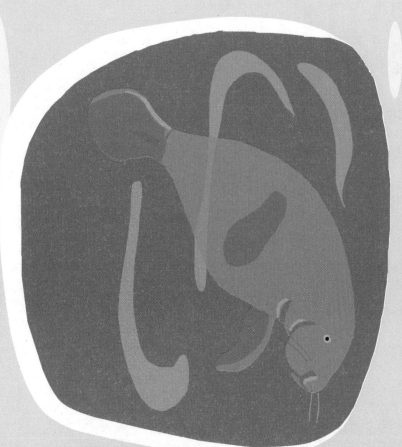

Scholastic 100 Words Kids Need to Read
by 3rd Grade, Word Group 1

Finally, we had enough bottles and cans,
thanks to all those manatee fans.
I asked my mom to write a check, then with a shout,
I stamped the envelope and mailed it out.

My cousin from Florida wrote to me,
He said, "Do you know about the manatee?
This animal is in trouble. It could die out.
We should adopt one. Would you help out?"

I told my cousin he could count on me.
I will tell everyone about the manatee.

We told everyone that we knew.
You would not believe how the pile
of cans and bottles grew!
Pretty soon it was up to my knee.
We were on a roll, to adopt a manatee.

6

I formed the M.T.W.B. group.
My friends all wanted to know the scoop.
I told them about adopting a manatee.
My friends all said they would gladly help me.

3

I wrote to my cousin about our plans to collect and recycle bottles and cans. We would save up all the money we got until we had enough to adopt.

"What's M.T.W.B. mean?" my cousin wrote in a letter. I wrote him back, "**Make The World Better!**"

The Manatee

We posted signs like these all about:

THE MANATEE

I'm gray-brown, with whiskers on my snout.
I swim slowly, while boats zoom about.
Would you protect me from being knocked out?

Word Talk

Use the words from the box to answer the riddles. Hint: You may need to use a capital letter.

Word Box

draw   hurt   laugh   talk   walk

Move your feet, don't be slow,

When you _____, you're on the go!

If you're skateboarding,

and hit the dirt.

Ouch! Watch out!

You might get _____ .

You can do it in person,

You can do it on the phone,

When you _____ to someone,

you're not alone.

Color a picture with a pencil or a crayon.

All you need is something to _____ on.

_____ out loud at least once a day.

That will keep a frown away.

Your Turn

Unscramble the letters to make a word.
Then it's your turn: Write a sentence using that word.

oh d l _____

_____

_____

k a l t _____

_____

_____

k a w l _____

_____

_____

t h r u _____

_____

_____

r a d w _____

_____

h u g a l _____

_____

_____

Define It!

Draw a line between each word and its definition. Then put the words in ABC order by numbering them from 1 to 8 in the boxes.

☐	walk	to carry
☐	hurt	to move on foot
☐	draw	to cause pain
☐	think	to make a picture
☐	bring	to have an idea
☐	laugh	to show joy
☐	talk	to say something
☐	buy	to get something at a store

Lily Pad Hop

Will you buy me a soda?

Will you held these flowers for me?

I used markers to drew that girl.

That joke really made me laugh.

Held on tight.

Do you like what I drew?

Held on tight.

I holded all my cards in one hand.

Look what I bought at the store.

We all laugh and laugh yesterday.

I hurt myself when I fell.

I hurted my hand playing ball.

I drawed this with crayons.

Draw a line from pad to pad to help the frog catch the fly. The frog can jump up and down or from side to side, but not diagonally. Only pads with correct sentences will allow the frog to move on.

I buyed that at the store.

I bought these boxes to your house for you.

He drawed that picture on the chalkboard.

I brang you some juice.

They had many thought about that.

Did you buyed that at the book store?

Think you for the present.

That was an interesting thought.

I brought all my cards to your house.

I want to buy a new radio.

I think I can do it now.

Do you hold hands when you cross the street?

I through about that idea.

Cross Your T's

Solve each riddle and then write the word in the correct space in the puzzle.

ACROSS

1. This word means to buy.

It ends in a **t**.

But it's in the past tense.

What can it be?

3. This word is so painful.

It ends in a **t**.

It makes you say, "ouch"!

What can it be?

4. This word means carried.

It ends in a **t**.

Don't confuse it with 1 Across.

What can it be?

DOWN

2. This word's an idea.

It ends in a **t**.

It's the past tense of think.

What can it be?

All in a Day

Time line

6 A.M. — 9 A.M.
9 A.M. — 12 P.M.
12 P.M. — 3 P.M.
3 P.M. — 6 P.M.
6 P.M. — 9 P.M.
9 P.M. — 6 A.M.

I have to walk home after school today.

If I fall out of bed, I will get hurt.

I drew that picture in my art class this morning.

I tried not to laugh when my brother spilled the juice at breakfast.

I bought pizza for lunch.

My father brought fish home for dinner.

Rhyme Time

Look at each set of pictures. Put an X on the picture whose name does not rhyme with the others. Then choose a word from the word box that rhymes with the names of the other two pictures.

_____

_____

_____

_____

_____

Think It Over

Draw straight lines between the present tense and the past tense words.

think	thought
draw	bought
buy	drew
hold	held

Write two sentences that tell what this man is thinking. Use a word from above in each sentence.

_____

_____

_____

_____

Now do the same thing for this boy.

_____

_____

_____

_____

Word Tree

Letter Box

o g h w r a

Use the correct letter from the letter box to finish each set of words on the word tree.

d __ e w

hu __ t

d __ a w

Missing Letter ___

t h __ u g h t

b __ u g h t

b r __ u g h t

Missing Letter ___

__ a l k

d r a __

d r e __

Missing Letter ___

__ o l d

__ u r t

__ e l d

Missing Letter ___

b r i n __

l a u __ h

b o u __ h t

Missing Letter ___

l __ u g h

t __ l k

w __ l k

Missing Letter ___

A Day at the Beach

Fill in the correct word that tells what's happening in the picture.

will draw

drawing

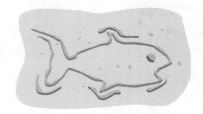

_____

will bring

bringing

_____

will _____

buying

bought

Mirror Riddles

Figure out the pattern to answer each riddle.
One word in each riddle is done for you.

How the girl got her paints all wet.

ehS werd reh htab

_____ drew _____ _____ .

Why the boy trained his dog to write notes.

ehT god saw oot yhs ot klat

_____ _____ _____ _____ _____ _____ talk.

What one card player said to the winner.

I tnaw ot dloh ruoy dnah

____ _____ ____ hold _____ .

If My Dog Could Talk

Use the words from the word box to finish the poem.

Word Box

think	bring
talk	walk
hold	buy

If I could teach

my dog to _____ ,

She'd say to me,

"Let's take a walk."

We'd _____ to the store,

And I'd _____ her a bone.

I'd buy myself

an ice cream cone.

Then my dog would say,

"Now let me _____ .

"Please get some water.

"I need a drink."

My dog would say

She needs fresh air.

She'd point to the park

And say, " _____ me there."

My dog might ask me,

To _____ her collar.

Then she'd say,

"I need a dollar."

So I'm glad my dog,

Can't talk today.

I'm not sure I'd like,

The things she'd say.

Phone Home

Find these words in the puzzle:
bought, bring, brought, buy, talk, held, think, thought, walk

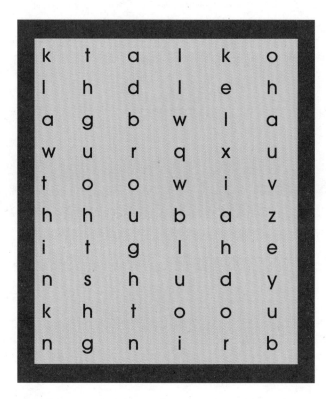

k	t	a	l	k	o
l	h	d	l	e	h
a	g	b	w	l	a
w	u	r	q	x	u
t	o	o	w	i	v
h	h	u	b	a	z
i	t	g	l	h	e
n	s	h	u	d	y
k	h	t	o	o	u
n	g	n	i	r	b

Write down the remaining letters.

__ __ __ __ __ __ __ __ __ __ __ __

Now unscramble them to solve this riddle.

Why was the monkey swinging from the telephone booth?

He _____ _____ _____.

Synonyms

Draw lines to connect the synonyms. Hint: Synonyms are words with similar meanings. Double hint: You won't need every word in the right column.

brought	boring
	chuckle
think	carried
	thought
talk	got
bought	consider
	hold
laugh	keep
	say

A Tense Mystery!

Color the past-tense verbs black.
Then color the present-tense verbs orange.

Going Home

Where does the artist live? Read the clues and follow the directions to find out.

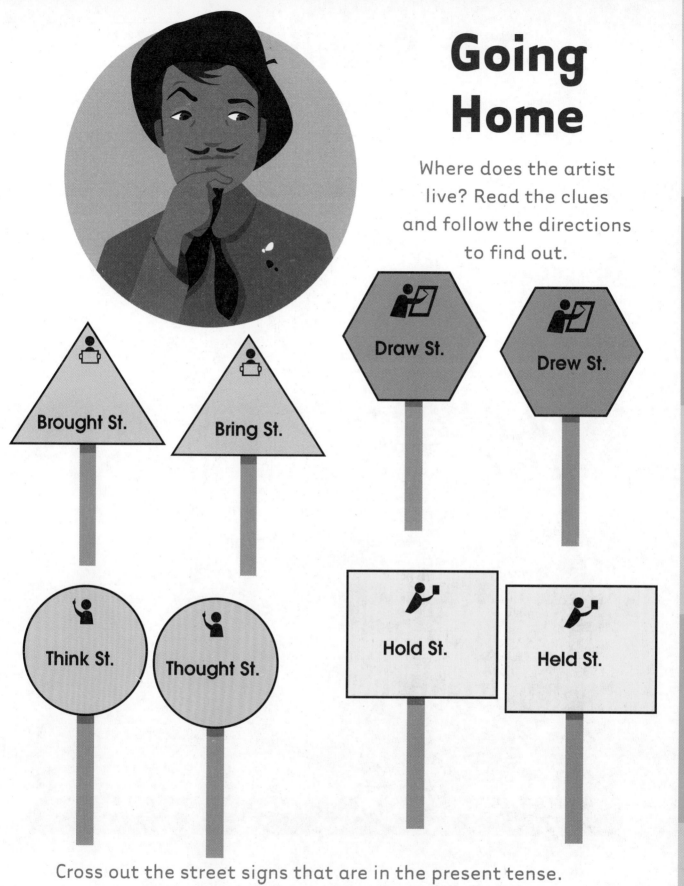

Brought St.

Bring St.

Draw St.

Drew St.

Think St.

Thought St.

Hold St.

Held St.

Cross out the street signs that are in the present tense.
Cross out the street signs that rhyme with fought.
Cross out the street signs that start with the letter **h**.
Circle the remaining street sign.
It is the one that tells where the artist lives.

The Spelling Bee

Help the bee get to his flower by moving it through the hive.
Put an X on all the words that are spelled incorrectly.
Then you'll see the correct path. Rewrite the words with
an X correctly on the lines below.

Fix the words you marked with an X.

_____   _____

_____   _____

School Day

Study the picture. Then circle **T** for true or **F** for false next to each sentence below.

1. The teacher is in the classroom.   T   F

2. The girl with a ponytail drew a bird.   T   F

3. There are six children in the classroom.   T   F

4. The girl in the yellow pants drew a bird.   T   F

5. A boy in green brought in his hamster.   T   F

6. A boy is holding a globe.   T   F

7. Two children are walking and talking.   T   F

Here's a Thought

Circle the correct word that finishes each sentence.

I am going to (brought, bought, buy, bring) that bicycle tomorrow.

I (brought, bought, buy, bring) that toy with me from home.

I (brought, bought, buy, bring) that pie to his house for dinner last night.

I plan to (brought, bought, buy, bring) that game for your birthday.

I (brought, bought, buy, bring) some juice at the store.

I (brought, bought, buy, bring) an ice cream cone at the park yesterday.

I will (brought, bought, buy, bring) you a glass of water.

I want to (brought, bought, buy, bring) my toy cars over to your house next weekend.

Write On!

Write your own sentences using the words you've been given.

_____ buy _____ .

_____ brought _____ .

_____ bring _____ .

_____ bought _____ .

Now choose one sentence and draw a picture to go with it.

Don't Waste the Water

Ms. Mung's class made signs telling people to save water. Use at least one word from the word box to make up your own sign about conserving water. Write the saying and then illustrate it in the poster below.

Word Box

bring	talk	walk
hold	think	

_____

_____

_____

_____

_____

_____

Please Hold!

How do you get from **talk** to **hold** in just five steps? Change one letter at a time. Each time you change a letter, the new word has to make sense. Hint: The middle word is done for you.

t a l k

___ ___ ___ ___

t o l l

___ ___ ___ ___

h o l d

Now go from **walk** to **hurt** in five steps. Try it.

w a l k

w a l ___

___ a l ___

h ___ ___ l

h u r t

Oops!

This homework is due tomorrow, but it has 9 mistakes. Check the spelling, punctuation, and grammar. Circle the mistakes.

When you buy an item at a stoor, due you ever thought about where that item comes from? Sum items travel a long way before you can bought them. think about your bicycle. The rubber for the tires start out as robber trees in the rain forest. Rubber sap is held inside the tree. People collect the sap and bring it all the way to town. Then it is bringed in a boat from the town to a factory where it is made into a tire for your bicycle. Be sure to wear a helmet when you ride, otherwise, you might get hert.

Planting Words

Put the words from the box in the right flower pot.

Word Box

bought	brought	laugh	talk	think	walk
bring	buy	laughed	talked	thought	walked

Past

_____
_____
_____
_____
_____

Present

_____
_____
_____
_____
_____

Tennis, Anyone?

Read the story. Then fill in the
missing words in the sentences below.

It's fun to learn to play tennis. First you learn the correct
way to hold your racket. You have to hold it tightly. When
you swing, you have to bring your arm all the way back.
Think about the way you are standing and how your arm
is moving. When the ball comes toward you, run, don't
walk. Stand firm. Hold your racket steady. Bring back your
arm. Now bring it forward. Smack! Hit the ball hard, right
over the net. Now you're playing like a pro!

To play tennis, first you have to learn t**h**e correct way to

_____ your racket.

When you swing, you hav**e** to _____ your arm

all the way back.

When playing te**n**nis, you should always try to _____

about what you ar**e** doing.

Balls come fas**t**. So you can't _____ to them slowly.

Sometimes you have to run.

Answer this riddle by writing the **red** letters
in order on the lines below.

What don't butterflies like about tennis?

___ ___ ___ ___ ___ ___

Bring Me a Brain

Read the story below and then answer the questions.

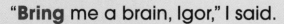

"**Bring** me a brain, Igor," I said.

I began to laugh. My creation was almost finished. Soon my monster would **walk** and **talk**. At least that's what I thought.

You can't just go out and **buy** a brain. Igor **brought** a head of cabbage to me instead. I got so angry that I yelled at him. I think I **hurt** his feelings.

Hold on there! I thought to myself. I've got it! Even if I can't use a store-**bought** brain, I **think** I know where I can get one.

"Oh Igor. . ." I said, as I **held** out my hand to him. I began to **laugh** again. But Igor was smarter than I thought. He ran for it—and took his brain with him.

Rats!

Which blue word is a synonym of stroll? _____

Which blue word means **to carry**? _____

Which blue word is the past tense of bring? _____

Which blue word is a homophone of bye? _____

Which blue word rhymes with half? _____

Which blue word rhymes with gold? _____

Which blue word means **to communicate**? _____

Which blue word is an antonym of **heal**? _____

Which blue word rhymes with wink? _____

Which blue word is a synonym of **purchased**? _____

Which blue word is the past tense of hold? _____ **Word Group Two** 67

What's the Story?

Use these words: **walk**, **talk**, **laugh**, **bring**, **buy**, to write a story about this giant.

You should write at least 5 sentences. Don't forget to add a title and your name.

_____

by _____

_____

_____

_____

_____

_____

_____

_____

_____

_____

The Giant Beetle

Replace the underlined words with their synonyms from the word box.

Today I <u>got</u> a new action figure. He's a giant beetle. I have wanted

_____

to <u>get</u> him ever since I saw him on TV. The giant beetle has sticky legs so

_____

he can <u>grasp</u> onto trees and poles. The minute I had him, I <u>carried</u> him

_____   _____

right home and took him up to my tree house. Then, I <u>wondered</u> about

_____

what to do with him. I could throw him out of the tree house and see if he

could climb back up. I didn't want to <u>damage</u> him. Instead, I <u>placed</u> him

_____   _____

against the tree house. He climbed to the top of the tree

house and then dropped right into my lap. It was so funny,

it made me <u>chuckle</u> out loud. I believe I might try him

_____

out in my sister's room tomorrow. I'm sure he would like

to <u>stroll</u> around her bed!

_____

Word Detective

Use the words in the word box to solve the clues.
You can only use each word once.

Word Box

bought	buy	laugh	think
brought	hold	talk	walk

Find the past tense of buy. _____

If you take the letter **h** out of this word, you have the

opposite of young. _____

Find the word that rhymes with bath. _____

Find the word with the silent **l**. _____

Find the word that rhymes with taught. _____

Find the word that comes before **tall** and after **tail** in the

dictionary. _____

Find the word that is the present tense of thought.

_____

Find the word that is the homophone of by.

_____

Last Laugh

Fill in the missing letters to finish the words.

br ___ ___ ght

b ___ ___ ___ ___ t

___ ___ ough

lau ___ ___

___ ___ ough ___

Word Group 2 Answer Key

41 walk; hurt; talk; draw; Laugh

42 hold; talk; walk; hurt; laugh; draw

43 match words with definitions;
8; 4; 3; 7; 1; 5; 6; 2

44–45 see right

46 see right

47 draw lines as directed

48 X on: crayon; bird; teeth;
fishtank; boy; cow;
write: draw; hurt; bring; think;
buy; drew

49 think/thought; draw/drew; buy/bought; hold/held; answers will vary

50 w; g; o; r; a; h

51 drew; buy; brought

52 She drew her bath. The dog was too shy to talk.
I want to hold your hand.

53 talk; walk; buy; think; Bring; hold

54 see right; He was on hold.

55 brought/carried; think/consider; talk/say; bought/got; laugh/chuckle

56 picture is a monarch butterfly

57 **Present Tense:** draw; bring; hold; think;
Rhymes with Fought: thought; brought;
Starts with H: held; hold; circle Drew St.

58 thought, brought, laugh, think, buy

59 1. F; 2. F; 3. T; 4. T; 5. F; 6. T; 7. T

60 circle: buy or bring; brought; brought; buy; bought; bought; bring; bring

61 answers will vary

62 answers will vary

63 tall; told; wall; hall; hurl

64 circle: stoor; due; thought; Sum; bought; think; robber; bringed; hert

65 **Past:** bought; brought; laughed; talked; thought; walked
Present: bring; buy; laugh; talk; think; walk

66 hold; bring; think; walk; The net

67 walk; bring; brought; buy; laugh; hold; talk; hurt; think; bought; held

68 answers will vary

69 bought; buy; hold; brought; thought; hurt; held; laugh; walk

70 bought; hold; laugh; walk; brought; talk; think; buy

71 ou; ough; en; gh; tht

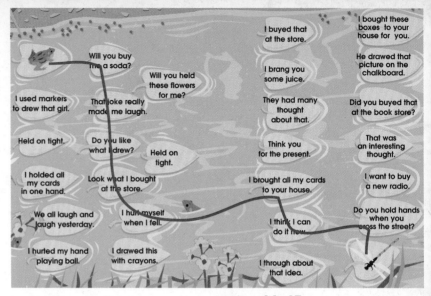

pages 44–45

page 46

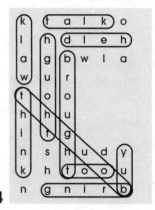

page 54

"Mom, Dad," said Julia when she got home from the party. "I think we need to talk."

Julia's mother and father gave each other a look.

"Honey," said Julia's dad. "I thought we already talked about this. We are having a baby."

"That is what I want to talk about," said Julia. "I think we should buy a cat instead."

8

······ fold & assemble ······

1

The New Baby

Written by Kathryn McKeon
Illustrated by Jackie Snider

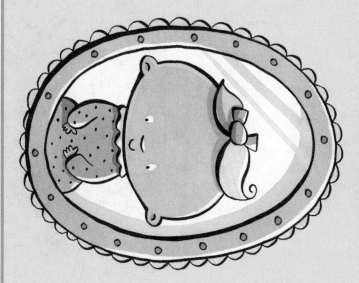

Scholastic 100 Words Kids Need to Read by 3rd Grade, Word Group 2

"Good idea," said Kayla. "Just hold on tightly to his leash."

Julia wanted to walk, but Spot raced around the yard dragging Julia behind him. "Aaaa!" she screamed. Kayla's mother ran outside. "Are you hurt?" she asked Julia.

"I think I'm okay," Julia said. Spot dug a hole, spraying mud all over everything.

7

On Monday Julia's mother went to the store and bought two rattles and a stuffed teddy bear.

On Tuesday Julia's father brought home a big blue stroller and a green high chair.

On Wednesday Julia watched two delivery men bring a white crib up the stairs.

"Mom, Dad," said Julia. "I think we need to talk."

2

On Saturday Julia went to Kayla's birthday party. Julia brought the present she had bought for Kayla and a bone for Kayla's dog, Spot.

At the party Spot gobbled up part of the birthday cake. Then he started barking so loudly it was hard to think.

"Can I take Spot for a walk?" Julia asked Kayla.

Julia's mother and father gave each other a look.

"Honey," said Julia's dad. "I thought we already talked about this. We are having a baby."

"That is what I want to talk about," said Julia. "I think we should buy a dog instead. I promise to walk him."

"You can walk the new baby in the stroller," said Julia's mother.

The next day at school Julia's teacher asked everyone to draw a picture of their family. Julia drew a picture of herself, her mother and father, and a big brown dog. In the picture, Julia held on to the dog's leash.

"Your parents bought you a dog?" asked Julia's friend Kayla.

"Not exactly," Julia answered.

That night Julia listened to her parents laugh and talk about baby names.

"Mom, Dad," said Julia. "I think we need to talk."

She gave them the picture she drew in school.

"We are not going to buy a dog," said Julia's mom.

"We are having a baby."

"But I already have a name for the dog," said Julia. "His name is Sam."

Word Search

Find these words in the puzzle below: **above, around, below, far, fly, going**

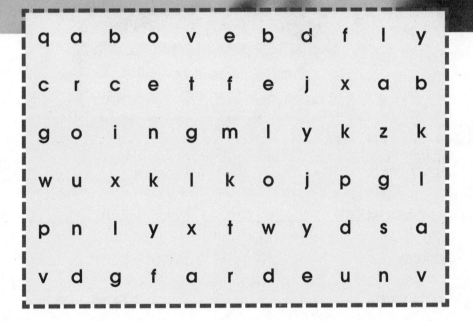

q	a	b	o	v	e	b	d	f	l	y
c	r	c	e	t	f	e	j	x	a	b
g	o	i	n	g	m	l	y	k	z	k
w	u	x	k	l	k	o	j	p	g	l
p	n	l	y	x	t	w	y	d	s	a
v	d	g	f	a	r	d	e	u	n	v

How many of these words have 1 syllable? _____

How many of these words have 2 syllables? _____

Around and Around

Use the words from the word box to finish the poem.

Word Box

above	below	fly
around	far	going

I jump on

And almost _____ .

I go low

And I go high.

I go up

And I go down.

I go in circles

All _____ .

I go up _____ .

I go down _____ .

Where I am _____

I don't really know.

But when I am done

Here's what I've found.

I never go _____

On my merry-go-round.

Up in the Tree

Circle **T** if the sentence is true, **F** is the sentence is false.

The girl is above the boy.	T	F
The boy is below a bird.	T	F
The flowers go all around the bottom of the tree.	T	F
The tree is by the fence.	T	F
The rope is tied around a branch.	T	F
A bird is flying above the tree.	T	F
The sun is coming through the clouds.	T	F
It is raining all around the tree.	T	F

A Wild Day!

Fill in the blanks before you read the story.
Then read your funny story aloud!

You'll never guess what I saw at the _____ yesterday.
place

A _____ was swinging from the monkey bars. I saw him
type of animal

climb up the ladder until he was above the _____. When
noun

he got to the top, he took _____ out of his bag and
plural noun

began throwing them at the children below. He thought it was

very _____ . The _____ laughed and
type of feeling   same animal

laughed. But the children didn't like it at all. I had to go because it was

time to _____ . So I didn't see what happened next.
a thing you do at home

But I heard it was really wild!

The Garden

Draw lines to the correct boxes to show what stays above ground and what goes below ground in a garden.

Below   Above

Letter Round-up

Follow the directions to find
the missing letters.

1. The letter is around the corner from the pigs. ____

2. The letter is behind the cow and below the door. ____

3. The letter is below the bell. ____

4. The letter is right below the weather vane. ____

5. The letter is far above the tallest tree. ____

6. The letter is through the meadow, in front of the umbrella. ____
7. The letter is very close to the owl. ____
8. The letter is behind the cloud. ____
9. The letter is above the shovel. ____
10. The letter is around the dog's collar. ____
11. The letter is above the farmer's nose. ____

Now put the letters you found in order to answer this riddle.

What did the chick do when he found out the fox

was near the chicken house?

___ ___ ___ ___   ___ ___ ___   ___ ___ ___ ___
 1   2   3   4   5   6   7   8   9 10 11

Farm Fresh

Unscramble the words. The letters underlined in red will spell the farmer's favorite breakfast food.

felw   ___ ___ ___ ___

wobel   ___ ___ ___ ___ ___

yver   ___ ___ ___ ___

gingo   ___ ___ ___ ___ ___

wrog   ___ ___ ___ ___

sode   ___ ___ ___ ___

fra   ___ ___ ___

wegr   ___ ___ ___ ___

Write the letters underlined in red in order on the lines below to answer the question.

What was the farmer's favorite breakfast?

Farm fresh ___ ___ ___ ___.

Flower Power

Fill in these flowery rhymes to solve the crossword puzzle.

I had a little flower garden

Where the butterflies would hunt.

There was a fence __ __ __ __ __ __ it.

1 across

And a wooden bench in front.

Each day I watered every plant.

And when that job was __ __ __ __.

2 down

I climbed up on my wooden bench.

And sat under the sun.

I watched the birds when they sang.

I watched them when they __ __ __ __.

2 across

I watched the flowers start out small.

And I watched them as they __ __ __ __.

3 across

Why did I love my garden so?

__ __ __ __ __ __ __ there is one

1 down

thing I know.

It feels just right to sit around.

And watch my garden __ __ __ __.

3 down

Search and Scramble

Unscramble the words and then circle them in the puzzle below.

vboea _____

hdbnie _____

nedo _____

yfl _____

lwoeb _____

wgro _____

a	g	r	f	o	p
g	b	e	l	o	w
e	l	o	y	p	o
n	v	r	v	a	r
o	r	d	o	e	g
d	n	i	h	e	b

Day and Night

Draw a line to connect the word
on the left with its opposite.

above	walk
shrink	far
ahead	below
coming	behind
near	going
run	grew
shrunk	grow

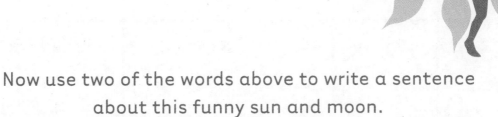

Now use two of the words above to write a sentence
about this funny sun and moon.

_____

_____

_____

Around the Block

Follow the directions to draw a map of your neighborhood.

	1	2	3	4	5	6
A						
B						
C						
D						
E						
F						

Draw your friend's house in box F2.

Draw your school so that it covers D2 and E2.

Draw a bicycle path through the center of the boxes from F1 to A1.

Draw a candy store in box B3.

Draw a video store in box C4.

Draw a firehouse so that it covers E4 and F4.

Draw your house in box C6.

Draw a highway so that it covers A2 to A6.

Draw a park so that it covers D4, D5, and D6.

Draw a mall so that it covers B5 and B6.

Draw a hospital so that it covers E5, E6, F5, and F6.

Now use three of the words from the word box to write a sentence that tells your friend how to get from her house to your house.

Word Box

| around | above | behind | below | through |

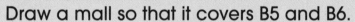

_____

_____

_____

_____

Rhyme and Write

Word Box

far	grow
fly	flew
done	very

Write the word from the word box
that rhymes with each group of words.

sun, one, bun _____

ferry, berry, library _____

car, jar, star _____

pie, eye, my

_____

hoe, blow, toe

_____

shoe, zoo, two

_____

From Acorn to Oak

The wind has blown this book apart and all the pages are mixed up.
Put the pages in order by numbering them from 1 to 7.

It rained. Water spread below the dirt and reached the seed.

Finally, the little acorn grew to be a new oak tree with little acorns of its own.

The little acorn hung on a big oak branch, far above the ground.

One day, the little acorn fell to the ground and landed behind the big oak tree.

A chipmunk found the acorn above some leaves. It cracked open the shell and buried the seed deep below the dirt.

The seed sprouted. Its stem poked up above the ground.

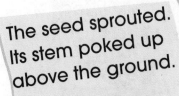

The plant grew and grew.

Monarchs Rule

Circle the 10 mistakes in this research report.

The Long Trip

Each year, thousands of monarch butterflies take a verry long trip. They flying from Canada to Mexico. They goes very far. Sometimes they fly thru stormy weather and they have to flew below the storm clouds. It's not an easy trip, but it's amazing to watch them as they flies through the air. They zip behind clouds and a round trees. Duz anyone really know why they make this very long trip? Yes. It is so they can lay their eggs. Then knew monarch butterflies will grew.

It's a Mystery

Fill in the sentences below with **did**, **do**, **does**, or **done**. Hint: You may need to use capital letters.

The Problem:

The new basketballs are missing. They were last seen in the school gym, which was locked. There is only one small window high above the floor. Nobody knows how anyone could have gotten in or out.

Your Mission:

Interview the basketball coach to see what he knows.

_____ you see anyone in the g**y**m yesterday?

Who _____ you think we should talk to?

Has anything like this ever been _____ bef**o**re?

Wh**e**n _____ you last see the basketballs?

On which side _____ the window usually open?

_____ you give anyone the **k**eys to the gym?

Wh**e**n _____ you usuall**y** go home?

When _____ you leave last night?

Now that you've asked the questions, you're ready to solve the mystery. Put the highlighted letters in order below to find out who took the basketballs.

__ __ __ __ __ __

Decode the Code

Use this code to figure out the saying. Hint: You may need to use capital letters.

a	b	c	d	e	f	g	h	i	j	k	l	m
1	2	3	4	5	6	7	8	9	10	11	12	13

n	o	p	q	r	s	t	u	v	w	x	y	z
14	15	16	17	18	19	20	21	22	23	24	25	26

An Ancient Saying in the Forest

```
20  8  5    2  9  18  4    11  14  5  23
T   h  e    b  i  r   d    k   n   e  w

8  5    23  1  19    7  15  9  14  7
h  e    w   a  s     g  o   i  n   g

20  15    7  18  15  23    2  21  20    8  5
t   o     g  r   o   w     b  u   t     h  e

4  9  4    14  15  20    11  14  15  23
d  i  d    n   o   t     k   n   o   w

8  15  23    6  1  18    8  5
h  o   w     f  a  r     h  e

23  15  21  24  4    6  12  25
w   o   u   l   d    f  l   y
```

Where?

Circle the letter of the sentence that describes each picture.

a. The girl is above the grass.

b. The girl is below the grass.

c. The girl is far away from the grass.

a. The boy is in front of the dog.

b. The boy is behind the dog.

c. The boy is above the dog.

a. The bird is above the flag.

b. The bird is behind the flag.

c. The bird is below the flag.

a. The bicycle is in the school.

b. The bicycle is on the school.

c. The bicycle is around the corner from the school.

a. The kitten is behind the cat.

b. The kitten is in front of the cat.

c. The kitten is above the cat.

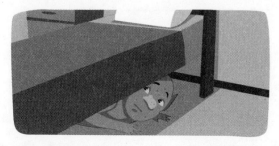

a. The monster is above the bed.

b. The monster is in front of the bed.

c. The monster is below the bed.

Batter Up

Write the direction words in one circle
and the action words in another.

Direction Words　　　　　　　　**Action Words**

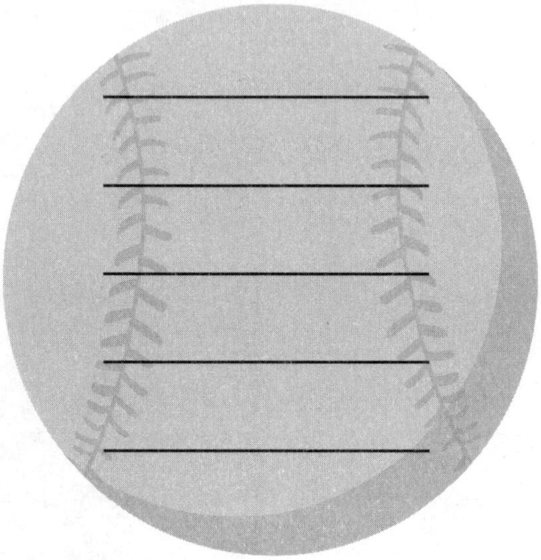

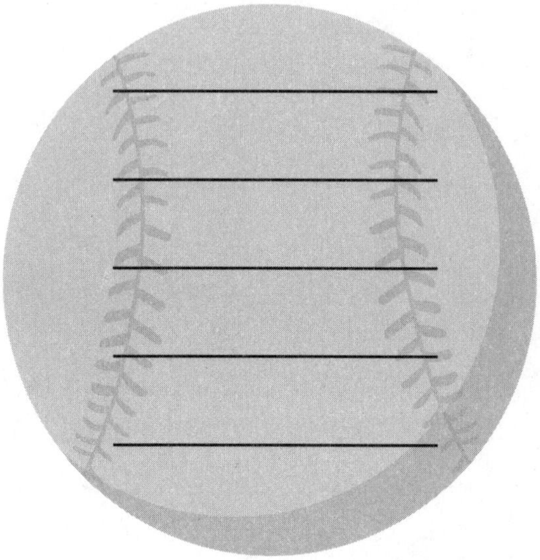

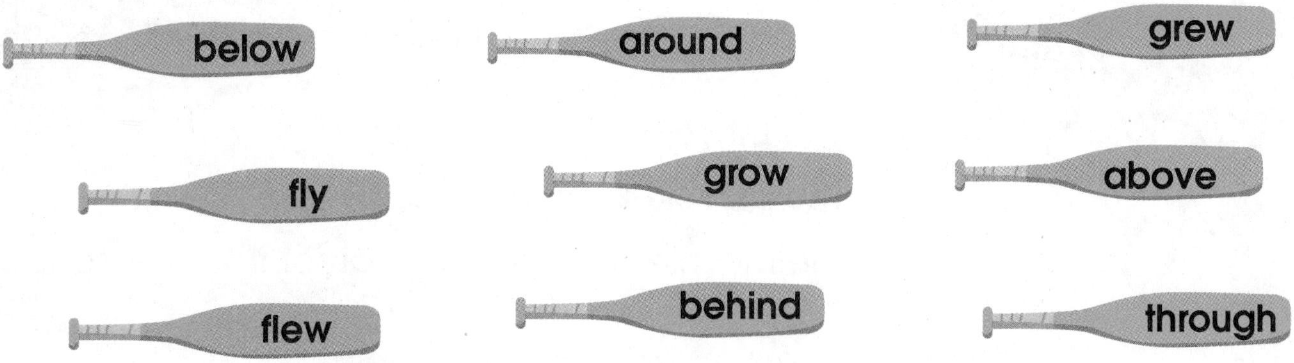

_____　　　　　_____

_____　　　　　_____

_____　　　　　_____

_____　　　　　_____

_____　　　　　_____

below　　　　around　　　　grew

fly　　　　grow　　　　above

flew　　　　behind　　　　through

Now use at least one word from each circle
to write a sentence about a baseball game.

_____

_____

_____

_____

Math Code

Use the code to figure out the number value of the words in the problems below. Then solve the problems.

a = 1   b = 2   c = 3   d = 4   e = 5   f = 1   g = 2   h = 3   i = 4
j = 5   k = 1   l = 2   m = 3   n = 4   o = 5   p = 1   q = 2   r = 3
s = 4   t = 5   u = 1   v = 2   w = 3   x = 4   y = 5   z = 1

Show why it is twice as good to be **done** than to **do**.

d o n e = _____   d o = _____

The difference between **done** and **do** is _____ .

What is worth more, **above** or **below**?

a b o v e = _____
b e l o w = _____

_____ by _____

How much more is **flew** worth than **fly**?

f l e w = _____   f l y = _____

The difference between flew and fly is _____ .

What is the difference between **grow** and **grew**? _____

g r o w = _____   g r e w = _____

How much are these words worth?

a r o u n d = _____
a b o v e = _____
b e l o w = _____

Now write them in value order of first, second, and third.

1 _____
2 _____
3 _____

If each letter value was worth one penny and you paid 25 cents for the word **through,** did you pay, too much, too little, or the right amount?

t h r o u g h = _____

Circle one:

too much   too little   right amount

Antonym Pairs

Pair up the sneakers. Draw lines between a word and its antonym. Hint: Antonyms are opposites—and not all the sneakers are part of a pair!

behind

shrink

grow

near

far

up

going

gone

above

ahead

coming

below

tall

Tell Me a Story

Write a story.
Here are your characters: you, a robot.
Here is the time: the year 3000.
Here are some words to include:
going, **fly**, **flew**, **above**, **below**.
Write at least 5 sentences.
Be as funny or as wild as you like!

_____

_____

_____

_____

_____

_____

_____

_____

_____

_____

Add a picture of the robot.

Ahoy!

Fill in the mystery letter in each set of words to answer the riddle.

5. v e ___ y
a ___ o u n d
g ___ e w
Mystery Letter ____

1. b e ___ o w
f ___ y
f ___ e w
Mystery Letter ____

2. g ___ i n g
d ___ e s
d ___ n e
Mystery Letter ____

3. f l e ___
g r e ___
g r o ___
Mystery Letter ____

4. a ___ o v e
___ e l o w
___ e h i n d
Mystery Letter ____

6. g o ___ n g
b e h ___ n d
t h ___ n k
Mystery Letter ____

7. ___ o e s
___ o n e
___ i d
mystery letter ____

8. ___ o i n g
___ r e w
___ r o w
Mystery Letter ____

9. b ___ h i n d
b ___ c a u s e
b ___ l o w
Mystery Letter ____

Now write the mystery letters in order on the lines below to answer the riddle.

What were the captain's least favorite words?

____ ____ ____ ____ ____ ! ____ ____ ____ ____

All About Earth

Earth is a spinning ball in space. It spins around very fast. Why don't you feel dizzy? It's because you are spinning around with the earth.

Our home planet is made of up many layers. Above Earth, there are layers of gas and chemicals called the atmosphere. Above the atmosphere is outer space. Below the earth's surface are different kinds of rock and metal layers.

No one knows for sure what Earth's inner core is like. That's because no one has ever gone to the center of the earth! But scientists who study the earth have ideas about what's inside its core. Many people believe that very hot liquid and solid iron make up this core. The iron twirls around and creates a magnetic pull.

Earth spins around very fast means it moves:

○ a. slowly

○ b. pretty quickly

○ c. extremely quickly

Where is Earth's atmosphere?

○ a. above the earth

○ b. inside the earth

○ c. in outer space

Which word in this story means the same thing as **under**?

○ a. above

○ b. magnetic

○ c. below

Where in the dictionary would you find the word **grow**?

○ a. between great and grew

○ b. between hello and icicle

○ c. between grew and hard

What do scientists believe makes up the earth's core?

○ a. very hot iron

○ b. the earth's atmosphere

○ c. they have no idea

Another word for **done** is

○ a. started

○ b. meal

○ c. finished

How Big?

Draw lines between the picture and the word or words that best describe it.

fast, very fast

little, very little

small, very small

tall, very tall

big, very big

Who Threw That Throw?

Circle the correct word to finish each sentence.

The night before our big game I almost wore a hole (through, threw) the rug by pacing back and forth. I was so nervous!

My team met before the game and we went (through, threw) all of our plans one more time. Then the umpire shouted: "Play ball!"

Our pitcher, Madeline, (through, threw) a fast ball and struck out the batter. Then the other team got a hit off her next throw. Madeline (through, threw) and (through, threw) , but the other team kept getting hits. Soon our team was down, 2–0.

My teammates munched on popcorn in the dugout. I was too nervous to eat, but they went (through, threw) three whole bags. At the bottom of the ninth inning, the game was tied, 3-3. It was my turn at bat. Bases were loaded. I stepped up to plate. The pitcher (through, threw) the ball. Strike one. The pitcher (through, threw) the ball again. I swung low. Strike two. The pitcher hurled the ball. I saw it flying (through, threw) the air. I swung the bat. Contact! The ball flew (through, threw) the field. It was a home run! We won! Our coach (through, threw) great after-game party!

Fishy Graph

Look at the picture. Fill in the bar graph to show how many animals are in the picture.

How many are **above** the surface of the water?

How many are **below** the surface of the water?

How many are **behind** a shell?

How many are going **through** a doorway?

	Above	Below	Behind	Through
6				
5				
4				
3				
2				
1				

Just Because

Re-arrange the letters to make 5 new words from the word **because**. The pictures will give you clues.

See

Sea

Scab

Case

Sauce

Now think of 3 more words you can make.
Hint: They don't have to be picture words.

Sub   usa   Use

Hoot! Hoot!

Write the number that matches the sentence
ending with the sentence beginning.

Sometimes an owl can _____

Some owls are endangered ___

Owls grow very quickly
from _____

Owls can see a mole _____

When an owl sees a mouse,

_____

1. it swoops down from above

   and grabs it.

2. eggs into birds of prey.

3. because their habitat is being

   taken away.

4. moving on the ground very far away.

5. hear a mouse moving below the snow.

Easy As . . .

Test your alphabetical skills.
First, put these words in ABC order:
**hold, bring, bought, drew, talk,
buy, thought, walk, draw, brought,
held, laugh, think, hurt.**

1. _____

2. _____

3. _____

4. _____

5. _____

6. _____

7. _____

8. _____

9. _____

10. _____

11. _____

12. _____

13. _____

14. _____

Now circle the correct answer.

In a dictionary, which would come first:

bring or **brought**?

Which would come second: **held** or **hold**?

Which would follow the: **think** or **thought**?

Word Group 3 Answer Key

77 see right; 2; 4

78 fly; around; above; below; going; far

79 F; T; F; T; T; T; F **page 77**

80 answers will vary

81 **above:** tree; flower; bird; bug **below:** roots; mole; mouse

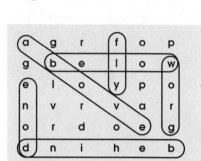

page 77

82–83 flew the coop

84 flew; below; very; going; grow; does; far; grew; eggs

85 behind; done; flew; grew; because; grow

86 above; behind; done; fly; below; grow; see right

87 above/below; shrink/grow; ahead/behind; coming/going; near/far; run/walk; shrunk/grew; answers will vary

page 86

88–89 answers will vary

90 done; very; far; fly; grow; flew

91 tk with final art

92 circle: verry; flying; goes; thru; flew; flies; around; Duz; knew; grew

93 Did; do; done; did; does; Did; do; did; a monkey

94 The bird knew he was going to grow, but he did not know how far he would fly.

95 a; b; c; c; a; c

96 **Direction Words:** above; around; behind; below; through; **Action Words:** grew; grow; fly; flew; answers will vary

97 9; below by 2; 3; none; 13; around = 18, above = 15, below = 17; 1. around; 2. below; 3. above; circle too much

98 behind/ahead; grow/shrink; far/near; going/coming; above/below; below/above

99 answers will vary

100 1. l; 2. o; 3. w; 4. b; 5. r; 6. i; 7. d; 8. g; 9. e; low bridge

101 c; a; c; a; a; c

102 draw lines to match text to pictures

103 circle: through; through; threw; threw; threw; through; threw; threw; through; through; threw

104 see right

105 cab; base; ace; bee; bus; answers will vary

106 5; 3; 2; 4; 1

107 1. bought; 2. bring; 3. brought; 4. buy; 5. draw; 6. drew; 7. held; 8. hold; 9. hurt; 10. laugh; 11. talk; 12. think; 13. thought; 14. walk circle bring; hold; think

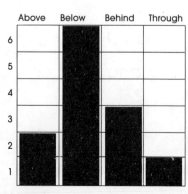

page 104

Different kinds of cicadas stay below ground for different amounts of time. Some cicadas come above ground every two or three years. Some come up every 13 or 17 years. Every 221 years, something amazing happens. All the cicadas come above ground at the same time and start to drum. What a sound!

fold & assemble

THE
SOUNDS
OF
CICADAS

written by Anne Schreiber

Scholastic *100 Words Kids Need to Read by 3rd Grade, Word Group 3*

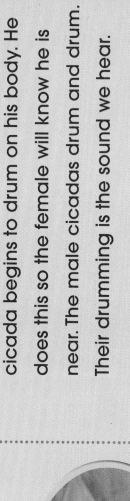

On warm summer days you might suddenly hear a sound all around. It sounds like tiny birds peeping. The sound grows. It's above, below, behind you, in front of you, all around you.

What just flew by?

It's the cicadas!

The cicada grew thin wings behind its back. Now it can fly to a nearby tree and it can look for a mate. The male cicada begins to drum on his body. He does this so the female will know he is near. The male cicadas drum and drum. Their drumming is the sound we hear.

After many years, the cicada is done growing. It crawls above the ground and looks for somewhere to rest. It might climb a tree or even a telephone pole. It breaks through its shell for the last time and becomes an adult.

Cicadas are insects. Like all insects, they have three body parts and six legs. A cicada starts out life as an egg. The female cicada climbs up the trunk of a tree. She cuts through the tree and lays her eggs below the bark. Far above the ground, the eggs are safe to grow.

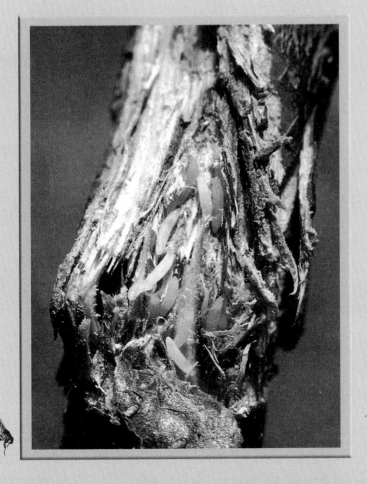

The cicada stays below the ground, sucking juices, for many years. The insect grows and grows. All around the cicada's body is a hard outer shell. Because the outer shell does not grow, the cicada gets too big for it. When this happens, the cicada breaks through the shell and grows a new one. It does this five times while living below the ground.

The eggs grow and hatch. A very small cicada breaks through the egg and falls to the ground below. The small insect burrows below the leaves and soil. It is going underground to look for a tree or plant root. Once it finds a root, the cicada starts doing what it does best—sucking juice.

Know Where You're Going

Use the words from the word box to finish the sentences below. The number of lines will give you clues.

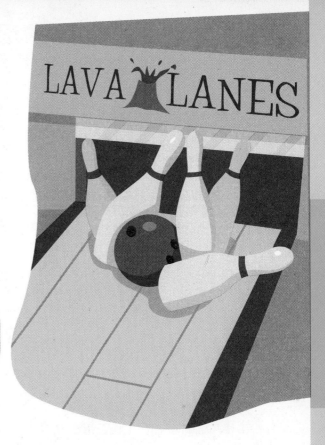

Word Box

left	light	right	wrong

Go straight down to the ___ ___ ___ ___ ___
                                          1

on Main Street.   Make a ___ ___ ___ ___ ___

turn onto Main Street and go three blocks. Then turn

___ ___ ___ ___ at the stop sign. Go three more
      2

blocks and turn ___ ___ ___ ___ again. You will

see an Enter and an Exit sign for Lava Lanes. Drive

___ ___ ___ ___ ___ into the parking lot.

Be careful! Don't go the ___ ___ ___ ___ ___ way!
                                      3

How did you bowl?

Look for the numbers below some of your answers in the story.
Fill in the matching letters below to see how many pins
you knocked down with your first ball.

___ ___ ___
 1   2   3

Turtle Test

This passage has 7 mistakes. Read the passage and circle all the mistakes. Pay attention to spelling, punctuation, and capital letters.

Sea Turtles

The sea turtle is a reptile that has adapted to life in the water. It lives most of it's life in the open ocean. Even so, the sea turtle must return to land every yere to lay egg's. In fact, females allways return to the same beach to lay their eggs. wons the sea turtle hatches her eggs, the sea turtle hatchlings. Must find their own way to the sea.

Now write the circled word as they should appear in the sentences.

_____

_____

_____

_____

_____

_____

I Wish

Fill in the blanks with words from the word box to tell how much you want your wish to come true!

Word Box

just	may
light	must

Star __ __ __ __ __, star bright,

First star I see tonight,

I wish I __ __ __

I wish I might.

I wish my wish comes true tonight!

You __ $\overline{2}$ __ $\overline{1}$ __ $\overline{3}$ __ $\overline{5}$
get your wish tomorrow!

So you $\overline{4}$ __ __ __
not have any sorrow!

Look for the numbers beneath some of the letters in your answers above. Then fill in the matching letters to finish the sentence to find out what you wished for.

Something yummy in my $\overline{1}$ $\overline{2}$ $\overline{3}$ $\overline{4}$ $\overline{5}$!

June Joy

Read the story below. Use the words from the word box to fill in the boxes and finish the sentences.

Word Box

month   it's   wrong   just   start   year

June is my favorite ☐☐☐☐ of the ☐☐☐.

Do you know why? If you think ☐☐'☐ because June is

the ☐☐☐☐ of summer vacation, you're

☐☐☐☐☐. June ☐☐☐ happens

to be special to me because my birthday comes in June!

Complete the sentences below using some of the words from above.

1. There are 365 days in a _____.

2. February is the shortest _____.

3. Use **it** and **is** to make the contraction _____.

Dot to Dot

Put the words from the word box in ABC order. Start by writing the first word next to the dot with the number 1. Then connect the dots. Circle the word that shows what you drew.

Word Box

once	just	start	never	light	left	may
its	year	month	always	must	right	wrong

7 _____

8 _____

6 _____

9 _____

10 _____

5 _____

11 _____

4 _____

3 _____

12 _____

2 _____

13 _____

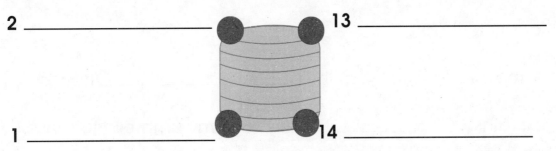

1 _____

14 _____

Word Search

Find these words: **always**, **left**, **may**, **must**, **once**, **start**, **year** in the puzzle.

a	m	u	s	t	o
b	l	o	s	r	n
u	q	w	t	d	c
t	m	m	a	y	e
y	e	a	r	y	t
l	e	f	t	z	s

Now, use the same words to finish these sentences.

1. Many fairy tales begin with "_____ upon a time . . ."

2. When it's time for recess, I _____ run outside.

3. A word that rhymes with **just** is _____ .

4. Every _____ my mom bakes me a cake

   for my birthday.

5. Some people write with their _____ hands.

6. If it rains, I _____ take my umbrella to school.

Letter Detectives

Find the missing letters in each set of words. Then use the letters to answer the riddle below.

1. on _____ e
   _____ ould
   _____ all

2. w _____ ong
   sta _____ t
   yea_____

3. j _____ st
   sho_____ld
   p_____ll

4. _____ay
   _____onth
   to_____orrow

5. _____ ust
   a _____ ong
   u _____ brella

6. _____ear
   ma_____
   toda_____

Write the missing letters in order here. _____

Now use the letters to answer the riddle.

Why did the cookie go to the hospital?

He was feeling _____ _____ _____ _____ _____ _____ !

Opposites Attract

Draw a line from a word under the big magnet to its opposite under the little magnet.

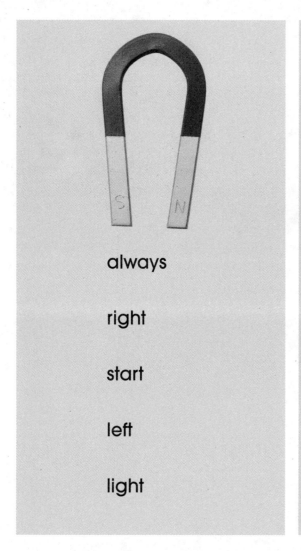

always

right

start

left

light

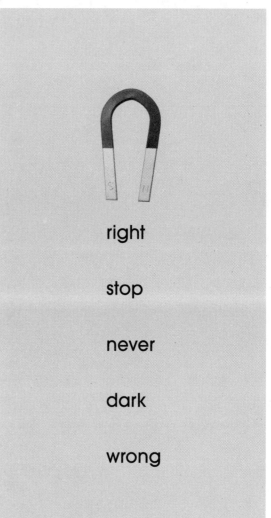

right

stop

never

dark

wrong

Fill in a pair of opposites for each sentence below.

1. Can you hold an ice cream cone with your _____

hand and the dog's leash with your _____ hand?

2. In the morning, it's _____ out and in the evening

it's _____ out.

Its or It's?

Use **it's** when you want to say **it is**. (**It is** my turn. **It's** my turn.)
Use **its** when you want to say a person or object owns something.
(The puppy wagged **its** tail. He owns his tail.)

Circle the word that finishes each sentence.

1. (Its, It's) time to go to soccer practice!

2. The dog licked (its, it's) puppies.

3. A robin usually sits on (its, it's) nest until the eggs hatch.

4. I wonder if (its, it's) going to rain.

5. A mother cat carries (its, it's) kittens in her mouth.

See You Later, Alligator

Use the words from the word box to fill in this passage.

Word Box

start   never   right   its   must   Once   Just

Did you know that if you had an alligator lying on your bed,

most of _____ tail would hang over the foot of the bed?

(_____ imagine if it snored!)

No matter how big an alligator is, it was very, very small at the

_____ . It came from an egg that wasn't much bigger than

the eggs you eat. The mother alligator builds a big nest and then

lays the eggs in it. _____ the eggs are laid, the mother

_____ _____ leave the nest. If the eggs are

left alone, an enemy could come along and eat them.

An alligator hatchling weighs more than a candy bar.

The hatchling can swim, climb, jump, and run around

_____ away!

Scrambled

Unscramble the letters in each egg to make the words from the word box.

g r h t i _____

e f t l _____

r w n g o _____

a m y _____

v e n e r _____

t t r a s _____

c e n o _____

Now choose two words from the word box and put them both in the same sentence.

_____

_____

Fill It Up

Use a letter from the pitcher to finish each word in a glass. Write the missing letter on the line.

_____ lways

_____ ay

_____ ight

_____ eft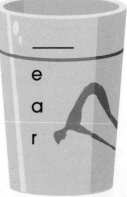

_____ rong

_____ ear

Color by Word

A - E - I - O - YOU can do it! Color by word
to finish this design! Follow the key and begin!

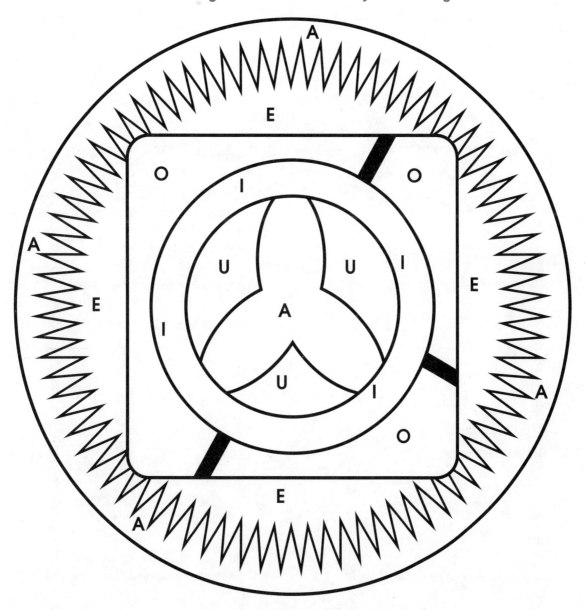

Key

Color all words with the letter a in red.
Color all words with the letter e in orange.
Color all words with the letter I in yellow.
Color all words with the letter o in green.
Color all words with the letter u in blue.
Color the places without any letters in purple!

Down the Hatch

Fill in the missing letter on the lines below to get down the hatch. Every time you change one letter, you make a new word. Look at the example below to see how to get from **bead** to **peek**.

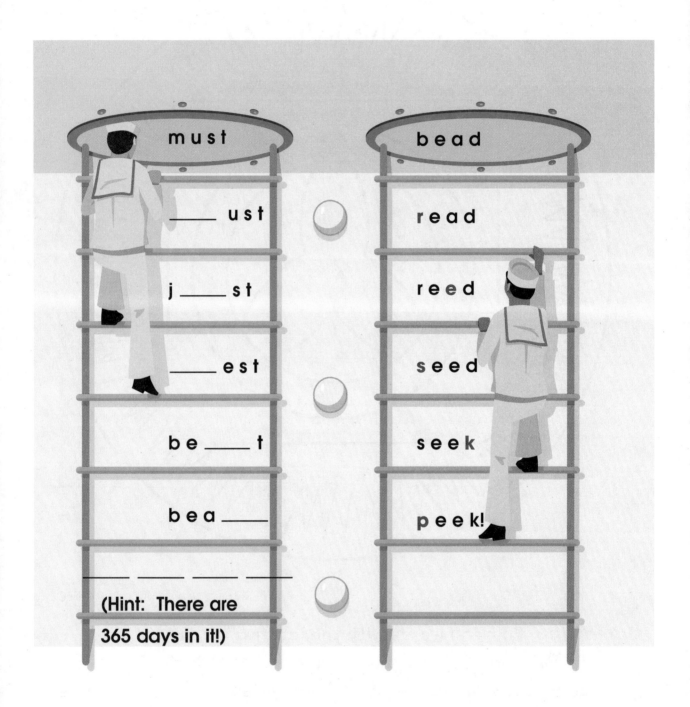

m u s t

_____ u s t

j _____ s t

_____ e s t

b e _____ t

b e a _____

_____ _____ _____ _____ _____

(Hint: There are 365 days in it!)

b e a d

r e a d

r e e d

s e e d

s e e k

p e e k!

Words, Words, Words

Read the clues and fill in the words to finish the puzzle.

Across

1. Part of a year
2. Synonym for begin
4. It's the time it takes the earth to revolve around the sun
6. Opposite of right
8. It means not ever
10. This word shows possession

Down

1. It means you're allowed
3. Synonym for correct
5. It means forever
7. A synonym for one time
9. It's the past tense of leave

Summer Vacation

Have a friend read aloud the words under the lines and write down what you say. Then read your funny story out loud.

How I Spent My Summer Vacation

Claire and I sold lemonade at my _____ stand.
                                    a drink

It was the _____ , my favorite time of the year.
              season

That's because it stays light out longer and you can go to

_____ later. Claire and I always yelled,
       noun

" _____ lemonade for sale!" to all the
       adjective

_____ passing by. Once, we left the stand to deliv-
   plural noun

er to someone who stayed parked in a _____!
                                            noun

We always had fun, even that time the _____
                                            animal

knocked over all the lemonade. And we made money! It was a

_____ we'll never forget!
   same season

A Cheesy End

Help get the mouse to the cheese.
You can only pass through the correct sentences.

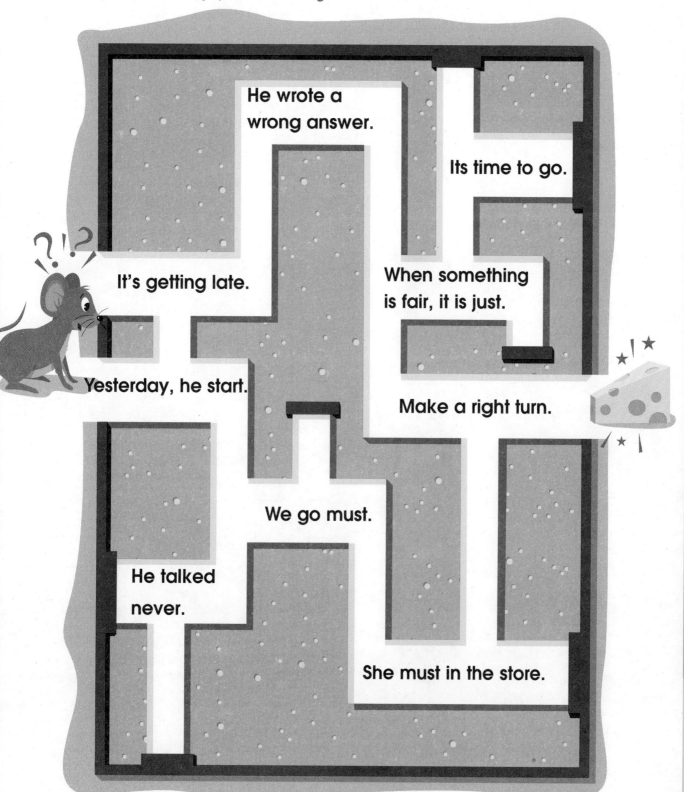

He wrote a wrong answer.

Its time to go.

It's getting late.

When something is fair, it is just.

Yesterday, he start.

Make a right turn.

We go must.

He talked never.

She must in the store.

Apples and Oranges

Make a fruit salad by drawing straight lines
between the words that rhyme.

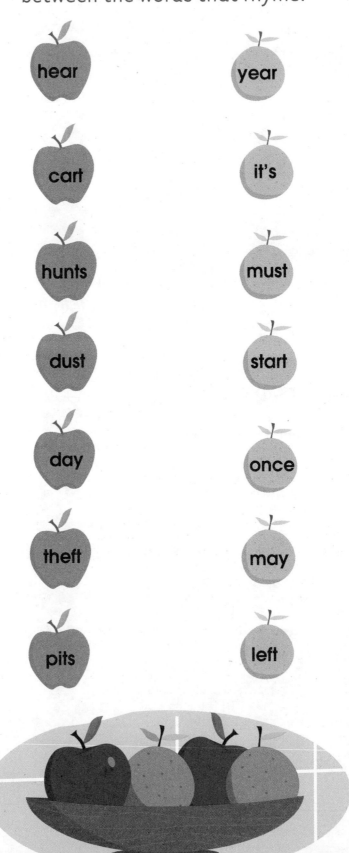

hear

year

cart

it's

hunts

must

dust

start

day

once

theft

may

pits

left

Always? Never!

Circle the things that you have done **once**. Underline the things that you **always** do. Put an X through the things you **never** do. Then put this information in the graph. The first one is done for you.

drank water

ate food

rode in a hot air balloon

went to the moon

went on a train ride

went for a tractor ride

took a horseback ride

went for a helicopter ride

went to a baseball game

been called to the principal's office

rode in a limousine

broke a bone

went ice skating

went ice fishing

How many times did you draw a circle? _____

How many times did you underline? _____

How many times did you draw an X? _____

Once	Always	Never
1.	drank water	
2.		
3.		
4.		
5.		
6.		
7.		
8.		
9.		

Cornered

Find the pairs of words in the word box that end in the same letter. Which pair fits in puzzle 1? Write in the words so they meet at the lower right-hand corner.

Now look at the example in puzzle 2. The word pair meets at the top corner. Try this yourself. For puzzle 3, choose a word from the word box. Write it across the bottom, then choose a new word that ends in the same letter and that will fit in the side boxes. Do the same thing for puzzle 4.

1

Word Box

just	start	once	it's
always	right	must	its

3

2

a	l	w	a	y	s

r

o

u

n

d

4

Get the Yolk?

Answer the jokes with words from the word box. Hint: One word is used twice.

Word Box

always	right	wrong
never	just	it's

Teacher: What would you get if you add 399 and 477 and 299?

Student: The ____ ____ ____ ____ ____ answer.

Student: Which is right? Five plus four is eleven or five plus four are eleven.

Teacher: They're both ____ ____ ____ ____ ____ .

Five plus four is nine.

Q: Why didn't the dog speak to his foot?

A: ____ ____ ' ____ not polite to talk back to your paw!

What did one math book say to the other?

I ____ ____ ____ ____ have a lot of problems.

What's the hardest part about taking a test?

Knowing the ____ ____ ____ ____ ____

answers.

Teacher: Luke, do you always thirst after knowledge?

Luke: No, I ____ ____ ____ ____ ____ ____ thirst after soda.

Why didn't the skeleton want to go to school?

His heart was ____ ____ ____ ____ ____ in it.

What's Up?

Analogies compare things in some way. Up is the opposite of down; in is the opposite of out. Use the words from the word box to help you finish these comparisons!

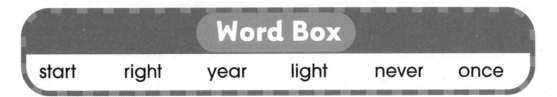

Word Box

start   right   year   light   never   once

Black is to white as **dark** is to _____ .

Together is to apart as **always** is to _____ .

Broken is to fixed as **wrong** is to _____ .

Day is to week as **month** is to_____ .

End is to beginning as **finish** is to _____ .

Second is to first as **twice** is to _____ .

What's on the Menu?

Unscramble the letters to find out what's on this word menu.

MENU

No. 1

Yum!

1

Get it!

A

👉 hotnm _____

👉 hitrg _____

👉 ryae _____

👉 reevn _____

👉 grwno _____

👉 slayaw _____

It's a Match

Draw a line from each word to a picture it rhymes with.

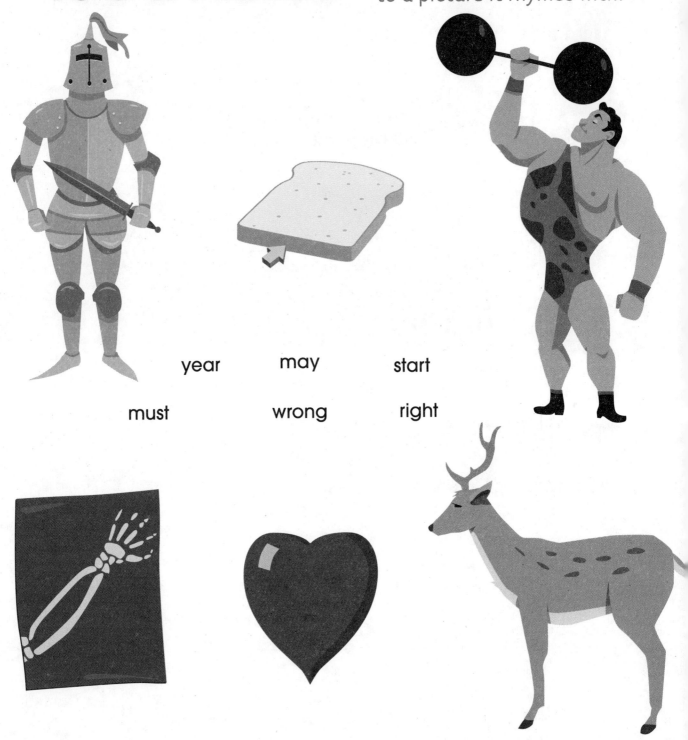

year   may   start

must   wrong   right

Now use a pair of rhyming words to write a sentence.

_____

_____

Sea Lions

Read the passage then circle
the answer to the questions.

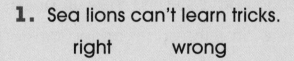

Sea lions perform in many circuses
and shows. It seems like it's easy for
sea lions to learn tricks. They're fed
a fish every time they do a trick the
right way. If they do it the wrong way,
they don't get a fish. Once sea lions
learn a trick, they get a fish every time
they do it. In the wild, sea lions spend
most of their time in the open waters of the
ocean, but sea lion pups are always born on
land. When a pup is about one year old, its mother
begins to teach it how to swim.

1. Sea lions can't learn tricks.
   right   wrong

2. Sea lions do not eat fish.
   right   wrong

3. Sea lion pups are born on land.
   right   wrong

4. Sea lions love the ocean.
   right   wrong

Here Comes the Sun

Read the passage. Then write **always** or **never**
to answer the questions.

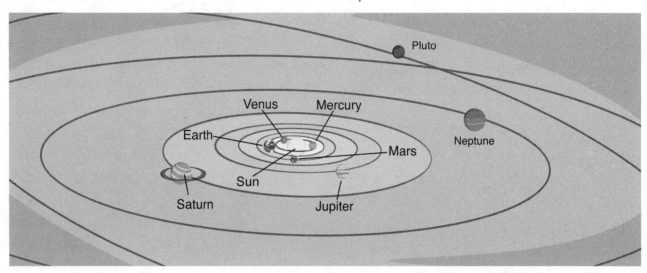

Our solar system is made up of nine planets, lots of moons, and lumps of rocks called asteroids. The Sun is the most important part of our solar system. It gives the planets their light and heat. Each planet goes around the Sun on its own invisible path called an orbit. Earth takes just over 365 days to orbit the Sun once. The time it takes for Earth to orbit the sun is called one earth year.

Many planets have moons that orbit them. Our moon takes about one month to go around the earth.

1. Does the Sun orbit Earth? _____

2. Does Earth orbit the Sun? _____

3. Does the Moon orbit Earth? _____

4. Does Earth orbit the Moon? _____

5. Does the Sun give us heat? _____

Now Hear This

Use the code to figure out each word and write it on the line.
Then use the circled letters to answer the riddle.

a	b	c	d	e	f	g	h	i	j	k	l	m
1	2	3	4	5	6	7	8	9	10	11	12	13

n	o	p	q	r	s	t	u	v	w	x	y	z
14	15	16	17	18	19	20	21	22	23	24	25	26

(2) 5 12 9 (5) 22 5 ____ ____ ____ ____ ____ ____ ____

(25) 5 1 (18) ____ ____ ____ ____

13 21 (19) 20 ____ ____ ____ ____

(15) (14) (3) 5 ____ ____ ____ ____

20 (15) 12 (4) ____ ____ ____ ____

How did the Vikings send secret messages?

____ ____ ____ ____ ____ ____ ____ ____ ____ ____ ____!
  2   25   14 15 18 19   5   3   15   4   5

Code Breaker

The first one is finished for you. The message is:
left to right! Hint: Each message has three words.

This jumbled message, **rortifgehlt**, is written
in inside-out code. To break the code:

Write the first letter, r, in the middle of a new line.	r
Write the next letter, o to the left of the r.	or
Write the third letter, another r, to the right of the first r.	orr
Write the fourth letter, t, to the left of the o.	torr
Write the fifth letter, i, to the right of the r.	torri
Keep writing letters, alternating from the	ftorri
left and right of the original message.	ftorrig
	eftorrigh
	leftorright

Follow the left—right pattern on page 140 to break
the code. The first steps are done for you.

1. nadtwhrgoinrg

n

an

2. osrynaewvlear

o

so

3. ohrtyneoamr

o

no

Awesome Acrostics

You can make an acrostic poem. Finish each word in the set using the first letters that are already printed. Try to use words that go together. The first one is done for you. Its theme is fall.

m -onth   y _____   l _____

O -ctober   e _____   i _____

N -ovember   a _____   g _____

t -urkey   r _____   h _____

h -oliday   t _____

Acrostic Fun, Too

You can make an acrostic out of your name.
Write your name vertically (the letters go down).
Then fill in a word across for each letter.
Use words about your favorite time of the year where you can.

Word Group 4 Answer Key

113 light; right; left; left; right; wrong; ten

114 it's; yere; egg's; allways; wons; Must; its; year; eggs; always; Once, must

115 light; may; just; may; must; tummy

116 month; year; it's; start; wrong; just 1. year; 2. month; 3. it's

117 1. always; 2. its; 3. just; 4. left; 5. light; 6. may; 7. month; 8. must; 9. never; 10. once; 11. right; 12. start; 13. wrong; 14. year; dots form a light bulb

118 see right for word search 1. Once; 2. always; 3. must; 4. year; 5. left; 6. may

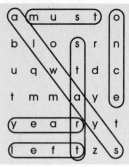

page 118

119 1. c; 2. r; 3. u; 4. m; 5. m; 6. y; crummy

120 always/never; right/wrong; start/stop; left/right; light/dark; 1. right, left (order may vary); 2. light, dark

121 1. It's; 2. its; 3. its; 4. it's; 5. its

122 its; Just; start; Once; must; never; right

123 right; wrong; left; never; may; start; once; answers will vary

124 answers will vary

125 color as directed

126 just/jest/best/beat/bear/year

127 **Across:** 1. month; 2. start; 4. year; 6. wrong; 8. never; 10. its;
Down: 1. may; 3. right; 5. always; 7. once; 9. left

128 answers will vary

129 Maze route: He wrote a wrong answer. It's getting late. Make a right turn. When something is fair, it is just. I may go to camp this summer.

130 hear/year; cart/start; hunts/once; dust/must; day/may; theft/left; pits/it's

131 answers will vary

132 1. its/it's; 3. right/start; 4. just/must

133 wrong; wrong; It's; just; right; always; never

134 light; never; right; year; start; once

135 month; right; year; never; wrong; always

136 year/deer; must/crust; may/X-ray; right/knight; start/heart; answers will vary

137 1. wrong; 2. wrong; 3. right; 4. right

138 1. never; 2. always; 3. always; 4. never; 5 always

139 believe; year; must; once; told; by Norse code.

140–141 1. right and wrong; 2. always or never; 3. month or year

142 answers will vary

143 answers will vary

It always feels just right for me
to dream beneath my willow tree.
I dream of where I'll be in a month or a year,
and hope my willowy willow still is here!

fold & assemble

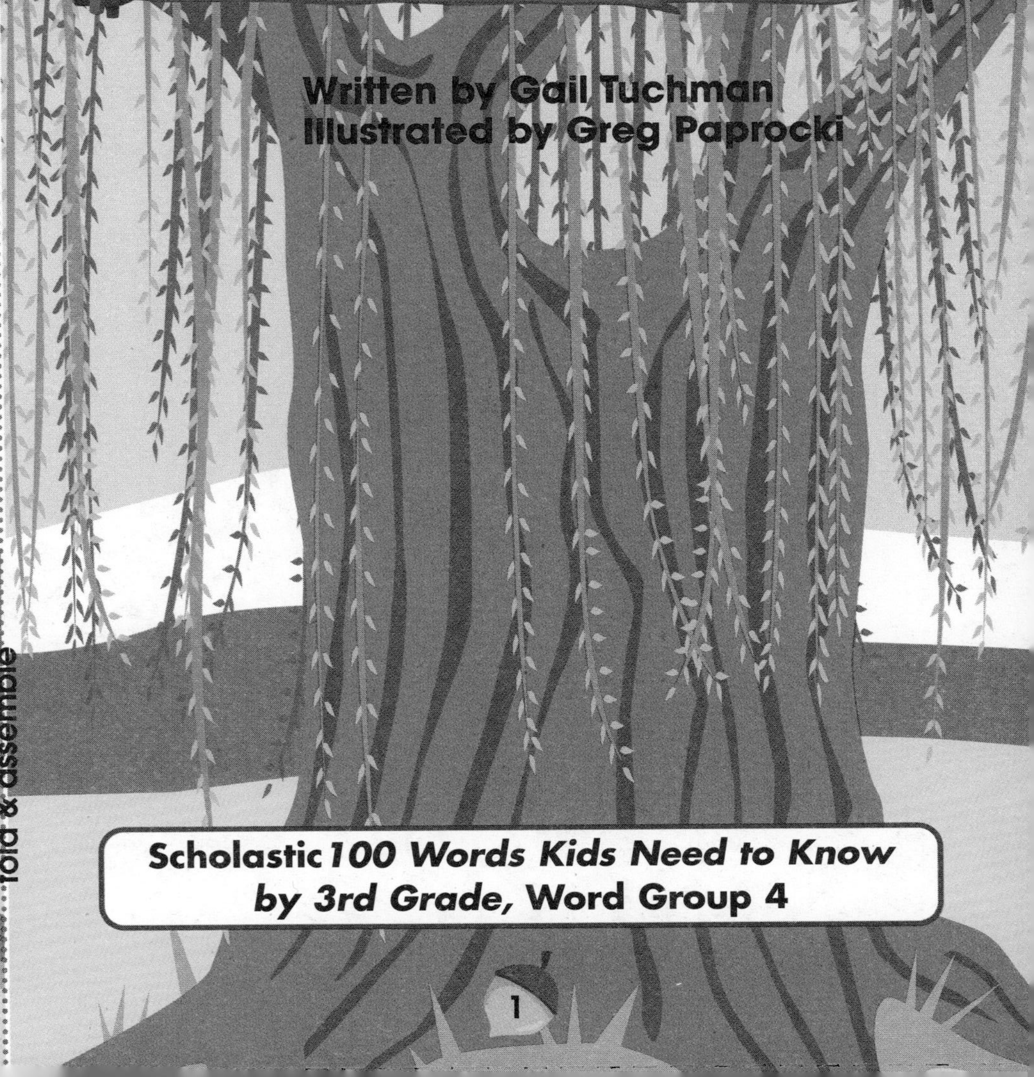

My Secret Hiding Place

Written by Gail Tuchman
Illustrated by Greg Paprocki

Scholastic 100 Words Kids Need to Know by 3rd Grade, Word Group 4

1

8

It always feels just right for me
to climb up into my willow tree.
I sit in a big branch and feel the breeze,
while long, green leaves tickle my knees.

Whenever I need a little space,
I head for my secret hiding place.

To the left, behind my house,
stands a weeping willow tree.
I must go under its hanging leaves,
then you will never see me.

It always feels just right for me
to laugh beneath my willow tree,
Once I start, I shake with glee.
Maybe it's just the feeling of being
free, beneath my willowy willow tree.

6

My secret place is just right for me.
It's warm and light and very cozy.
Nothing is ever wrong you see,
Under my willowy willow tree.

3

It always feels just right for me
to draw beneath my willow tree.
I draw an ant carrying its crumb around,
and a snake crawling on the ground.
I even draw a buzzing bee,
beneath my willowy willow tree.

It always feels just right for me
to read beneath my willow tree.
I may read about dinosaurs,
pirate ships, or people who explore.
It's fun to read a mystery
beneath my willowy willow tree.

What Are You Like?

Circle the word that finishes the sentence correctly.
Then underline yes or no to tell what you like.

I like to (call, called) my friends on the phone.   yes   no

I (found, find) it more fun to play video games with a friend.   yes   no

I would (many, much) rather play a game than watch a game. yes   no

I prefer a day (fill, full) of things to do with friends.   yes   no

I (extra, only) like (too, to) read a book once.   yes   no

I am the (kid, kind) of person who likes my room neat and tidy. yes   no

I (shall, said) be nine on my next birthday.   yes   no

Space Travel

Use the words from the word box to finish your spaceship checklist. You may use a word more than once.

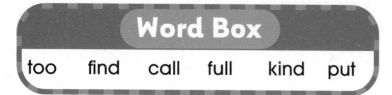

Word Box

too	find	call	full	kind	put

1. ____ ____ ____ ____ the ignition switch.
    1

2. Make sure the fuel tank

is ____ ____ ____ ____ .
   2

3. Make sure you have the right

____ ____ ____ ____ of space food.
    3

4. Make sure nothing is ____ ____ ____ heavy.
             4

5. ____ ____ ____ on your seat belt.
      5

6. ____ ____ ____ ____ the map that
   6

tells you how to get there.

7. Give your mom a ____ ____ ____ ____
                 7
to say good-bye.

Put the numbered letters in order
to find out what comes
after the checklist.

____ ____ ____ ____   ____ ____ ____
 7   3   6   5   4   2   1

The Computer Virus

A computer virus hit this email message!
Now there are 9 mistakes in it. Circle each of them.

Hi, Marcy,

Will you be around later this afternoon? If it's not too mchu trouble, I was hoping you could teach me how to use my new computer. I can't found any of my games, but my dad says he putt them on my computer this morning.If you can help me find the games, you can play them with me to. Its making me so mad, I want to put the whole thing up-on a shelf where I don't have to look at it. My mom thinks its funny that now that I have a computer, I want it to go awway. I only only wish I knew what was wrong. Could the memory be fully?

If you can't come over, please give me a caller anyway.

Thanks.

Gabbi

Spot the Antonyms

Antonyms are words that mean the opposite, such as **high** and **low**.
Circle the antonyms below .

full	write
tell	said
silly	funny
find	little
round	lose
lift	empty
pull	square
told	push
much	long

Skateboard Rules

Read the paragraph below.
Then fill in the correct bubble,
based on what you read.

Kevin loves to skateboard. His mom thinks this is fine, but there are some rules he has to follow. Kevin has to put on his helmet. He has to wear his knee pads, too. Kevin can only skateboard if he's finished his homework. He can't skate too far away. If he skateboards with friends and is going to be late, he has to call.

Kevin doesn't find these rules to be too hard. He loves to skateboard. If he has to follow a rule or two, that's the kind of deal he can live with.

	True	False
Kevin's mom doesn't mind that he skateboards, as long as he follows her rules.	○	○
Kevin doesn't like to skateboard much.	○	○
Kevin has to wear his helmet, knee pads, and a good luck charm, too.	○	○
Kevin has to finish his homework before skateboarding.	○	○
Kevin has to call if he's going to be late.	○	○

Storyland Mix-Up

An elf mixed up all the pages in the storybook. Read each sentence. Then write the letter for the sentence that would follow it.

1. Jack put the jar of magic beans on the table. _____

2. The first soup Goldilocks tasted was too hot. _____

3. The wolf sucked in his breath until his cheeks were full. _____

4. Hansel and Gretel were lost in the woods and far away from home. _____

5. Aladdin rubbed the magic lantern. _____

6. Snow White fell deep asleep. _____

A. The seven dwarves found her and brought her home
B. She tasted the second soup, but it was too cold.
C. Suddenly they came upon a sweet candy house.
D. The genie appeared.
E. Then he blew down the little pig's house.
F. He dreamed of how they might grow.

Alphabet Cereal

Find these words in the puzzle below: **pull**, **shall**, **found**, **call**, **find**, **away**, **full**, **round**, **too**, **put**, **upon**, **only**, **kind**, **much**

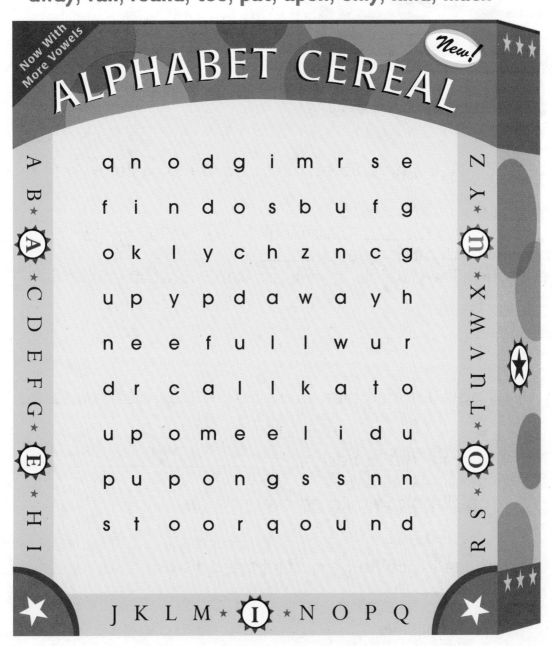

Write a sentence about your favorite cereal.
Use three of the words you circled.

_____

_____

_____

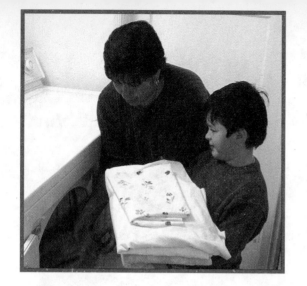

Laundry Jumbles

How do you do the laundry?
Unscramble the letters
in the jumbled words to learn.

uPt _____ _____ _____ the colored clothes and the white clothes in two piles.

OyIn _____ _____ _____ _____ wash whites with whites and colors with colors.

fndi Go through the pockets of your jeans to see what you can

_____ _____ _____ _____.

oto llfu Don't pack the machine _____ _____ _____ _____ _____ _____ _____

oto mhcu Be careful not to add _____ _____ _____ _____ _____ _____ _____

soap. Bubbles would go everywhere!

yawa Now turn the machine on and let the dirt wash _____ _____ _____ _____

llup tpu When it's finished, _____ _____ _____ _____ everything out and

_____ _____ _____ it in the dryer.

lcal Next time you can do it yourself and _____ _____ _____ _____ me

if you need help.

Sounds Delicious

Circle the letter next to the word that finishes the sentence. Write the word on the line.

1. Jack is the _____ one who didn't eat dessert.
   always - n; only - m

2. This block of cheese is square and that one is _____ .
   round - i; around - e

3. My soup is _____ hot to eat.
   to – w; too - c

4. Cathy says her cake won't taste right unless we _____ all
   found - a; find - e

   the right spices.

5. Don't fill my glass so _____ or I will spill it.
   fill – fl; full - cr

6. It's time for lunch, let's put our books _____ .
   away - i ; over - o

7. If I eat all these cookies I'm going to be _____ .
   full- s; fill- c

8. She was baking all day. I've never seen her bake so _____ .
   much - p; lots- l

9. I looked in 10 cookbooks for the recipe and I

   finally _____ it.
   find - a; found - i

10. If I _____ more sugar in, the cookies will be very sweet.
    put – es; pull - se

Now use the letters from your correct answers above
to find out what cats eat for breakfast.

___ ___ ___ ___
 1   2   3   4

___ ___ ___ ___ ___ ___ ___ ___
 5   5   6   7   8   9 10 10

One Down, Two to Go . . .

Using the words from the word box, write all the possible answers
to each clue until you get to the one correct answer.

1. It has four letters. _____ _____

_____ _____ _____

_____ _____ _____

_____ _____

It has four letters and has two repeating letters at the end.

_____ _____ _____ _____

It has four letters, ends in two repeating letters,

and means the opposite of push. _____

2. It's an action word.

_____ _____ _____

_____ _____

It's an action word in the present tense.

_____ _____

_____ _____

It's an action word in the present tense

that rhymes with foot. _____

3. It has five letters.

_____ _____ _____

It has five letters and rhymes with hound.

_____ _____

It has five letters, rhymes with hound,

and is the past tense of find. _____

4. It has the letter **o**

_____ _____ _____

_____ _____

It has the letter **o** and is two syllables.

_____ _____

It has the letter **o**, has two syllables, and rhymes with lonely. _____

5. It has one syllable. _____ _____

_____ _____ _____

_____ _____ _____

_____ _____ _____

It has one syllable and ends with a **d**.

_____ _____

_____ _____

It has one syllable, ends with a **d** and is the opposite of lose.

_____

Picture Clues

Use the words from the word box to finish the sentences. The pictures will give you clues.

Word Box

kind	much	away	call	pull	full

1. I put a rock on my newspaper

   so it wouldn't fly _____ .

2. I sat by the phone and waited

   for a _____ .

3. I kept eating cake

   until I felt _____ .

4. I want a new video game,

   but it costs too _____ money.

5. My baby sister likes to _____ my hair.

6. My grandmother says that

   I'm one of a _____ .

I Want It

Can you buy these items? Look at each price. Add up the money shown. Underline **too much** if you will get change when you buy the item. Underline **too little** if you won't have enough money to buy it. Underline **just right** if you have exactly the right amount.

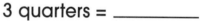

This costs 75¢

3 quarters = _____

too much   too little   just right

This costs $3.99

$5.00 + $1.00 = _____

too much   too little   just right

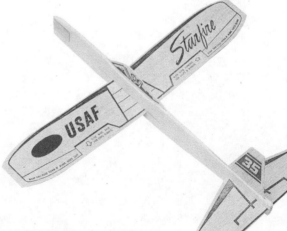

This costs 20¢

1 penny + 1 nickel = _____

too much   too little   just right

This costs $1.25

1 quarter + 1 dime + 1 nickel= _____

too much   too little   just right

Push and Pull

How many things can you think of that you **pull**?
How many things can you think of that you **push**?
Write their names on the lines.

Push

_____

_____

_____

_____

_____

Pull

_____

_____

_____

_____

_____

Shilly-Shally

Circle the words with the same last two letters as **shall**.
Then unscramble the underlined letters
in those words to solve the riddle.

k i n d   p u l l
c a l l   p u t
m u c h   f u l l
f i n d   o n l y

How the mice felt when the cat went on vacation.

____ ____ ____ y ____ ____ ____

Watch Out!

Replace the underlined words in the story below with words from the word box that mean the same thing.

Word Box

ask	found	much	put	too
find	kind	out	round	away

First locate _____ a base. Try to

find a plastic tray. The type _____

you throw out _____ is best. Now

find some clay. Place _____ the

clay on the tray and shape it into a mound.

Make a circle-shaped _____ hole

in the middle. Now fill up the hole half-way

with baking soda. Don't add more than you

need _____ _____ .

Find some vinegar. Once you have located

_____ it, mix it with food coloring

to make it look like lava. Now here comes

the fun part, so request _____ all

your friends over to look. Fill the hole with

vinegar. Boom. Your volcano will explode.

We Found Out

Find the smaller words in the big word.

found

Find four 2-letter words. _____

_____

_____

_____

Find one 3-letter word. _____

Find one 4-letter word. _____

shall

Find one 2-letter word _____

Find two 3-letter words. _____ _____

Find one 4-letter word. _____

find

Find two 2-letter words. _____ _____

Find one 3-letter word. _____

kind

Find one 2-letter word. _____

Find two 3-letter words. _____ _____

Rhyme Time

Circle each pair of rhyming words.

only	odd
pull	full
away	does
call	fall
much	many
shall	pal
put	putter
too	zoo
find	kind
round	found

Kick Off

Use these words: **call**, **pull**, **away**, **only**, **much**, **too**
to write your own football story.

_____

_____

_____

_____

_____

_____

_____

_____

_____

_____

_____

_____

_____

The Merry-Go-Round

Cross out all the vowels in the list of letters below.
Write what's left in order in the lines below
to solve the riddle.

r	a	i	o	n	i	d	e	o	n
i	d	a	a	r	e	n	u	o	d
n	i	d	o	e	r	n	e	u	d
s	i	a	h	o	g	s	a	e	o

Where does the merry-go-round go?

____ o u ____ ____   a ____ ____   ____ o u ____ ____

a ____ ____

____ o u ____ ____   ____ ____ e   g ____ ____ s!

Dog Tales

Use the words from the word box to finish the poem.

Word Box

away	found	kind	too
find	full	pull	upon

Last night I wished _____ a star.

But I think I went _____ far.

First I wished that I could _____

a pet dog that was sweet and _____.

But the next thing that I knew,

the puppies numbered 102.

The puppies began to push and _____.

My room was getting very _____.

I knew that if my mother _____

my room filled with all these hounds

I would be in a lot of trouble!

The puppies liked

to play and play. But I knew they could not stay,

so I wished they'd go _____.

But the next thing that I knew,

all my things had vanished, too!

So now all my things are gone.

That's the last star I'll wish upon!

Belonging

Write each word from the word box
under the correct heading.

Word Box

call	hat	put
find	kind	round
flat	mind	square
found	pound	
full	pull	

Rhyming Words

_____

_____

_____

_____

_____

_____

_____

_____

_____

Shape Words

_____

_____

_____

Verbs

_____

_____

_____

_____

_____

Out of the Past

Read the sentences below. Fill in the word that makes sense.

The archaeologist hoped to _____ old pottery from the past.
find   found

He had to work very carefully to _____ what he was looking for.
find   found

He started digging. In two days, he _____ his first object.
find   found

He got out his smallest tools. He wiped away the dirt

and dust on what he had _____ .
find   found

"What a _____ !" the archaeologist cried.
find   found

Puppy Love

Fill in the mystery letter that finishes each set of words.

____ p o n
p ____ t
m ____ c h
Mystery Letter: ____

r o u n ____
f o u n ____
k i n ____
Mystery Letter: ____

t o ____
r ____ u n d
____ n l y
Mystery Letter: ____

k i ____ d
f o u ____ d
f i ____ d
Mystery Letter: ____

____ u l l
____ i n d
____ o u n d
Mystery Letter: ____

Now unscramble the mystery letters to solve the riddle.

What the lost puppy wished he could be:

____ ____ ____ ____ ____

Two for Two

Fill in the blanks with **to**, **too**, or **two**.

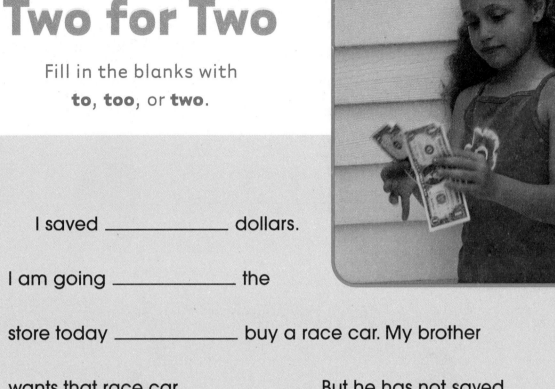

I saved _____ dollars.

I am going _____ the

store today _____ buy a race car. My brother

wants that race car, _____. But he has not saved

_____ dollars yet. If I have any change, I am

going _____ buy him something. I know

I won't have _____ much money left over

_____ spend, but I do want _____ get him

something. I think gum is only _____ cents at that

store. Maybe I'll be able _____ buy _____

pieces of gum. I'll buy one piece for him and one piece for

me, _____.

Get In Shape

Word Box

call	shall
pull	full

Write the word from the word box that fits best.

Make two new words. Change the vowel in two of the words above to **i**.

Rhyme Circles

On each line, put an X through the word that does not rhyme and circle the words that do rhyme.

too   much   drew

find   kind   found

shall   pal   call

find   round   found

shall   full   pull

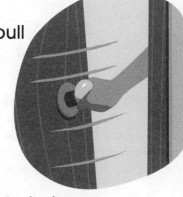

call   shall   fall

Make a sentence using two of the words you circled.

_____

_____

S-s-snake!

Follow the key to color in the snake.

upon

call

kind

put

full

much

round

Key:

Words that end in the letter **y** = orange

Words that rhyme with foot = yellow

Two syllable words that do not end with the letter **y** = blue

Words with the same ending sound as the word mill = red

Words that rhyme with the word **sound** = brown

Words that rhyme with the word mind = **black**

Words that have the same ending sound as the word peach = **purple**

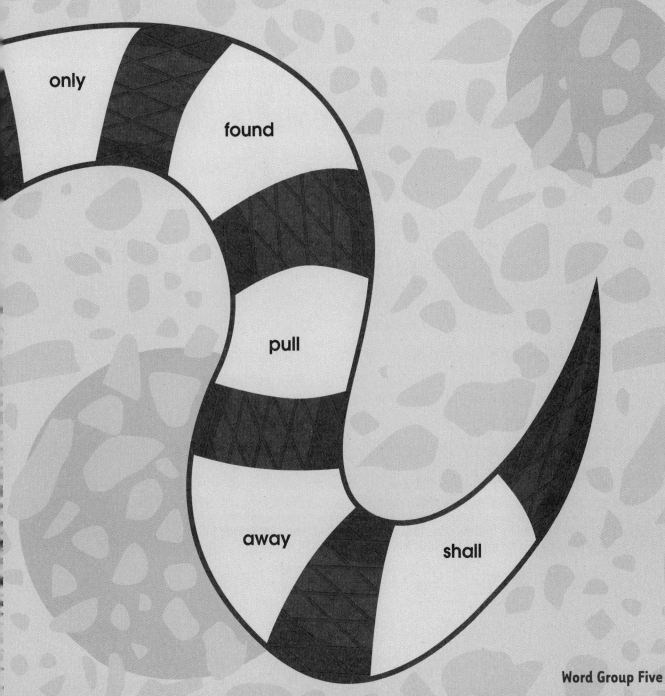

only

found

pull

away

shall

Word Group 5 Answer Key

149 call; find; much; full; only; to; kind; shall; yes/no answers will vary

150 1. Find; 2. full; 3. kind; 4. too; 5. Put; 6. Find; call; lift off

151 mchu; found; putt; to; up-on; awway; only; fully; caller

152 full/empty; much/little; pull/push; find/lose; round/square

153 true; false; false; true; true

154 1. F; 2. B; 3. E; 4. C; 5. D; 6. A

155 see right; answers will vary

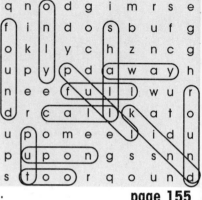

page 155

156 Put; Only; find; too full; too much; away; pull; put; call

157 1. only; 2. round; 3. too; 4. find; 5. full; 6. away; 7. full; 8. much; 9. found; 10. put; mice crispies

158–159 1. away, call, find, kind, much, only, pull, put, upon; call, full, pull, shall, pull; 2. call, find, found, pull, put; call, find, pull, put; 3. found, round, shall; round, found; found; 4. found, only, round, too, upon; only, upon; only; 5. call, find, found, full, kind, much, pull, put, round, shall, too; find found, kind, round; found

160 underline: 1. away; 2. call; 3. full; 4. much; 5. pull; 6. kind

161 $4.99 too much; 75¢ just right; 6¢ too little; 40¢ too little

162 answers will vary

163 circle: call, pull, full, playful

164 find; kind; away; Put; round; too much; found; call

165 **found**: do, of, on, no; fun: fund, fond; **shall**: as; all; has; hall; **find**: if, in; fin; **kind**: in; ink

166 circle: pull/full; round/found; call/fall; find/kind; shall/pal; too/zoo.

167 answers will vary

168 round and round and round she goes!

169 upon; too; find; kind; pull; full; found; away

170 **Rhyming Words:** find, kind, mind; found, pound, round; flat, hat; full, pull; **Shape Words:** flat, round, square; **Verbs:** call, find, found, pound, pull, put

171 find; find; found; found; find

172 u; o; d; n; f; found

173 two; to; to; too; two; to; too; to; to; two; to two; too

174 pill; fill

175 put an X on much; found; call; find; shall; shall circle: find/kind; full/pull; call/fall; round/found; shall/pal; too/drew

176–177 color as directed

The next day, Izzy tried to find his wallet one more time. He looked under his desk. There were not one, but two wallets!

Izzy ran downstairs. He hugged his mother and sister. "I found something even better than my wallet," he said. "I found out how kind my family is!"

Several months later Izzy found something else, too— his wallet! It was waiting for him just where Spot had left it.

8

1

Scholastic 100 Words Kids Need to Read by 3rd Grade, Word Group 5

WHAT IZZY FOUND

Written by Anne Schreiber
Illustrated by Valeria Petrone

That night, while Izzy slept, his sister snuck into his room. She put a new wallet under Izzy's desk. In it was all the money she had earned walking Spot. Then she tiptoed out.

A few minutes later, Izzy's mom came in. She too had bought a new wallet and filled it with money. She put it under Izzy's desk and quietly walked away.

Izzy finished raking. His bag was finally full. Only a few leaves were left on the ground. He put away the rake and leaned upon Mr. Thompson's bell. Mr. Thompson came out. He pulled two crisp dollar bills from his pocket and handed them to Izzy. Izzy put them into his pocket. "Thanks!" he called out. Then Izzy hopped upon his bike and headed home.

Izzy had planned to wake up early the next day and buy his new rocket. Instead, he spent much of the morning trying to find his wallet. He found many other things. He found bottle caps, treasure cards, round marbles, flat rocks, and curvy shells. But he did not find the wallet. Izzy's mom and sister felt sorry for him. Each one thought about what to do.

6

Izzy ran straight to his room and pulled the two dollars from his pocket. He took his wallet from behind his games. No one else will ever find it there, he thought. Izzy's wallet was full of coins and bills. Just as he was about to put more money in, he heard his mom call. Dinner was ready. Izzy washed up and ate with his family.

3

Izzy told his family that he had enough money to buy his model rocket.

"I'm getting the 100 Foot Deluxe model," he said.

"It can blast 110 feet in the air. It can do much, much more, too," he said.

After dinner Izzy went away to count his money again. That's when his mother heard the scream.

4

Izzy's mom and sister ran to his room. They found Izzy on the floor, peering under his desk. The wallet was gone. The only money left was the two dollars that he hadn't put away.

"Somebody found it and took it," Izzy cried. He glared at his sister.

"Don't look at me," she said. "I didn't do it."

"Did too," Izzy started to say, but his mom spoke up. "We shall get to the bottom of this," she said.

5

Half & Half

Put these words in alphabetical order: **ready**, **again**, **about**, **word**, **own**, **carry**, **sure**, **city**, **clean**, **though**, **warm**, **middle**, **live**, **which**.

1. _____

2. _____

3. _____

4. _____

5. _____

6. _____

7. _____

8. _____

9. _____

10. _____

11. _____

12. _____

13. _____

14. _____

How many of these words fall in the first half of the alphabet? _____

How many in the second half? _____

Strike Out

Cross out each ball that is the antonym, or opposite,
of the word in the bat.

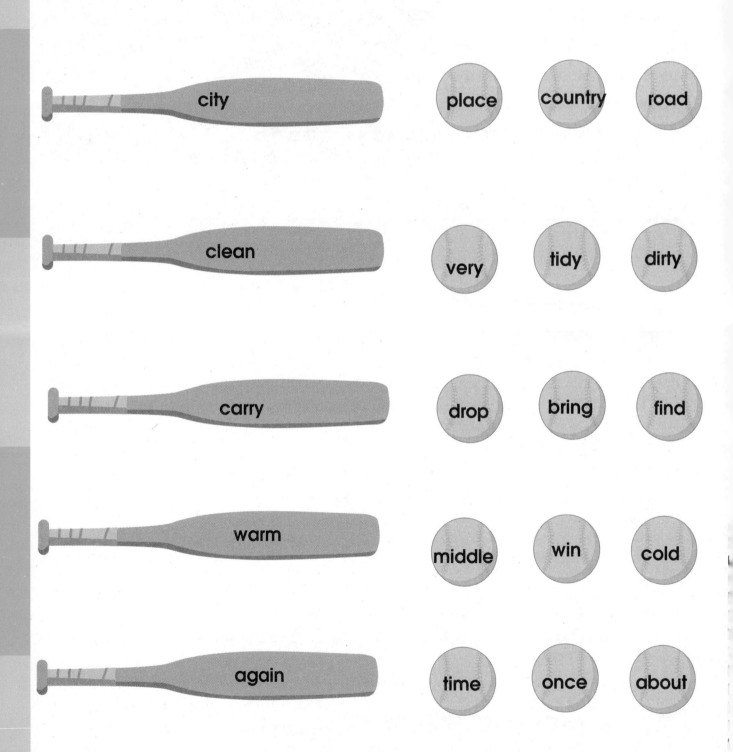

city — place, country, road

clean — very, tidy, dirty

carry — drop, bring, find

warm — middle, win, cold

again — time, once, about

The Story of Goldilocks

Replace the green words with words from the word box
that are synonyms, or mean the same thing.

Word Box

| again | clean | middle | own | sure | warm |

What happened between Goldilocks and the three bears was really

just a big misunderstanding. Goldilocks wasn't certain _____about

who lived in that house in the woods. All she knew was that it was cold

outside and that house looked not hot or cold _____ inside. She

also thought it looked tidy _____, and she wanted somewhere nice

to rest. After all, she wasn't in the center _____ of the city where she

could just pop into a hotel. Goldilocks didn't mean to cause a problem.

But the three bears did possess _____ that house in the woods and

they thought what Goldilocks did was just plain rude. One thing

Goldilocks and the three bears do agree on — Goldilocks will not visit

them another time _____.

How to Make Apple Pie

The steps in this recipe are all mixed up.
Fill in these missing words: **again**, **about**, **clean**,
middle, **own**, **ready**, **sure**, **warm**. Then write numbers
from 1 — 5 in the boxes to put the recipe in the right order.

☐ After you have rolled the pie crust,
wash the apples until you are
_____they are
_____. An adult can help
you peel and slice them.

☐ Last, have an adult help
you take the pie out of the oven.
It will be _____ and
delicious. Eat it with ice cream!

☐ The next day, take the pie crust out of the refrigerator. Roll it with a rolling pin if you _____ one. If not, use a jar. Roll the crust until it is thin. You may have to do this _____ and again.

☐ When the apples are sliced, put them in the _____ of the pie crust. Sprinkle it with sugar and put the pie in the oven.

☐ First make crust by mixing together _____ 1 cup of flour with about 1/3 cup of cold butter and about 3 tablespoons of cold water. Form it into a ball and refrigerate over night so that it is _____ to use when you make the rest of the pie.

Rhyming Puzzles

Draw lines between the puzzle pieces that form rhyming pairs.

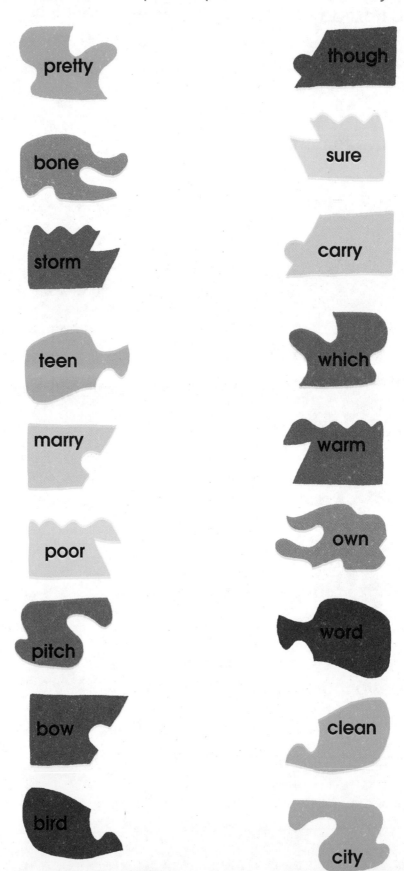

pretty

though

bone

sure

storm

carry

teen

which

marry

warm

poor

own

pitch

word

bow

clean

bird

city

Picnic

Write the words from the word box in one of the
parts of speech boxes to show which kinds of words they are.
Hint: One word goes in two boxes.

Word Box

carry   city   clean   live   warm   word

Nouns
(Thing Words)

_____

_____

Adjectives
(Describing Words)

_____

_____

Verbs
(Action Words)

_____   _____

_____   _____

Dig the Roots!

Write the root word for the underlined word in each
sentence and then find that root word in the puzzle.

Root Word

I was <u>living</u> in the city, but I moved to the country. _____

I <u>readied</u> myself for the test by studying. _____

Are you <u>warming</u> up the pizza from last night? _____

I once <u>owned</u> a mountain bike. _____

I can't talk now. I'm <u>cleaning</u> my room. _____

a	r	s	c	l	m	t	o
l	x	y	a	l	p	o	a
y	l	n	r	e	e	a	n
p	i	w	r	p	p	a	i
v	v	o	y	t	u	e	n
r	e	a	d	y	o	a	i
y	x	m	r	a	w	k	l
o	e	x	r	t	d	e	a

The Right Ending

Replace the underlined words with words from the word box that have the same meaning.

Word Box

| again | carry | clean | live | warm | word |

Each summer, we go to <u>dwell</u> _____ on a boat.

Most of the time, living on a boat is lots of fun. Sometimes it's

hard work. For one thing, we always have to keep everything

<u>tidy</u> _____ . Also, my brother and I argue about who

is going to <u>lift</u> _____ the water and food. Another

time, I wrote a poem about our boat. It got published in the

local paper. They liked my <u>groups of letters</u> _____ .

Now that I think of it, I'm ready to live on the boat <u>another time</u>

_____ next summer.

Own It!

Circle the word **own** as many times as you can find it.
The word may go up, down, sideways, or diagonally.

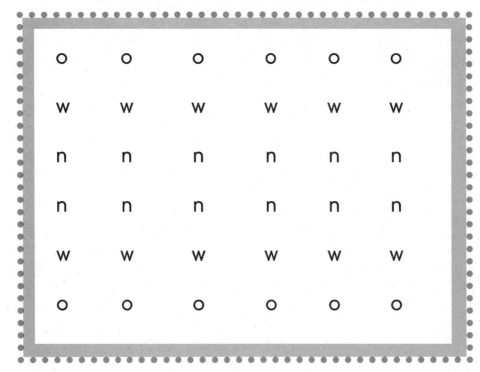

How many times could you find the word? _____

Which Witch?

Homophones are words that sound the same, but are spelled differently and mean different things Choose the correct homophone, **which** or **witch**, to finish each sentence.

I dressed up as a _____ last Halloween.

I don't know _____ color apple to eat.

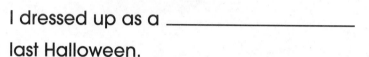

This story had a scary _____ who flew around on a broom.

_____ shirt do you like best?

Riddle in the Middle

Use the code to answer the riddles.

Riddle Code

a = @	e = #	m = 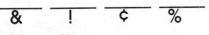	t = *
c = "	i = +	o = !	w = &
d = %	l = $	r = ¢	y = ^

I'm the apple in the pie.

I'm the hole in a fiddle.

I'm the core in an apple.

I am the

__   __   __   __   __   __
🍎   +   %   % $ #

I'm used inside sentences.

I like to be heard.

I'm made up of letters.

I am a

__   __   __   __ .
&   !   ¢   %

A nice summer day

For me is the norm.

I'm not hot and not cold

Instead I am

__   __   __   __ .
&   @   ¢   🍎

I'm full of buildings and people,

Postcards of me are pretty

I have cars, trains, and buses

I am the " + * ^

__   __   __   __ .
"   +   *   ^

Pyramids of Questions

Read the story about ancient Egypt. Then circle True or False to answer the questions.

Have you heard about the pyramids of Egypt? They are giant structures located right in the middle of the desert, outside the city of Cairo. Even though the people who built the pyramids lived thousands of years ago, they were excellent builders.

To build the pyramids, workers had to bring giant pieces of rock many miles. The rocks were too heavy to carry. They weighed tons! So the workers dragged the huge rocks. They crossed the warm, sandy desert again and again to do this. It was hard, dangerous, and tiring work.

Do you know why the pyramids were built? Ancient kings were buried there, along with some of the special things they owned.

The pyramids of Egypt were built long ago.	True	False
The people who built the pyramids were not very good at building things.	True	False
It was easy to build the pyramids.	True	False
The builders only had to carry giant pieces of rock across the desert one time.	True	False
The desert is a hot and sandy place.	True	False
The pyramids were built for the kings.	True	False
Another word for middle is center.	True	False

What's Inside?

The answer to the riddle is hidden inside the word in bold.
Use some of those letters and write your new word on the line.

Find the fruit in the **middle**.

____ ____ ____ ____

Find something you fish with in **word**.

____ ____ ____

Find the exit in **about**.

____ ____ ____

Find the body part in **warm**.

____ ____ ____

Find the greeting in **which**.

____ ____

Find a way to travel in **carry**.

____ ____ ____

In Orbit

Place the correct word from the word box inside the planet. Look for definition clues in the planet's moons!

no pollution

to tidy up

clear, pure

_____

Word Box

clean	own	warm
middle	sure	

not hot, not cold

to reheat

belongs to oneself

_____

to have

_____

equally distant from all sides

reliable

certain

central

_____

_____

positive

City Search

Circle each of the words on this list: **about, again, carry, city, clean, live, middle, own, ready, sure, though, warm, which, word**

```
b n w o a e l d d i m h
c e c o n a e l c l t g
a k r m r a w a i w h u
r b a u r d r v t d o o
r m o s s r e w y y u h
y i w u y e o d c d g t
w d n r t a n r l a h h
h d r e i d i o e e d c
i l s e c y a w a r m i
c e l i v e g a n r c h
h h t u o b a g a i n w
```

My Cousin and I

Read just the clues to a friend and fill in the answers. Then read the story aloud to see what you've written.

My favorite days are the long, warm days of _____ .
                                               season

Every year my cousin visits me in my _____ in the coun-
                       building

try. The things we are sure to do every summer are _____
                       verb

in the pond, eat lots of _____ , and ride our
               food

_____ into town. Sometimes, at night, we have a
  plural noun

barbecue out on the _____. When the fire is warm we are
               noun

ready to roast _____ . I have my own room, so my cousin
         plural noun

and I can stay up late _____ and reading books. In the
        verb ending in ing

morning we eat breakfast and brush our _____ and
                         body part

_____ . Then we are ready for the anything! Next
  body part

summer, I want to visit my cousin in the city where she lives. I think

that will be very _____ .
         feeling

There's a Monster in My Pocket!

Solve this monster crossword.

Across

2. Oh, no! Not _____ !

7. The monster is going to destroy our _____ !

8. Even _____ it looks mean, I think we should try to talk to it!

10. Is that its mouth in the _____ of its head?

13. I have only one _____ to say: "Help!"

14. Who's going to _____ up this mess?

Down

1. We better get _____ for a big mess.

3. What _____ the police? Can they help?

4. _____ way should we run?

5. It's getting kind of _____ around here.

6. I am not _____ what to do next.

9. I can't _____ that monster — it's too big!

11. See? The monster just wants to _____ in peace.

12. Get your _____ monster. This one is mine.

Word Windows

Draw a line from the street to the top floor window. True statements are like opened windows. You can pass through them. False sentences are like closed windows. You cannot pass through.

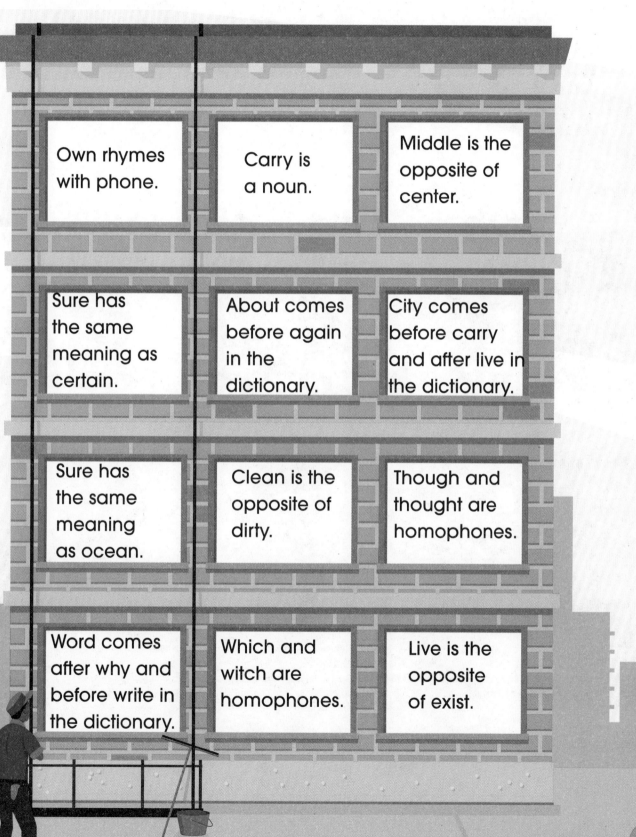

Own rhymes with phone.

Carry is a noun.

Middle is the opposite of center.

Sure has the same meaning as certain.

About comes before again in the dictionary.

City comes before carry and after live in the dictionary.

Sure has the same meaning as ocean.

Clean is the opposite of dirty.

Though and thought are homophones.

Word comes after why and before write in the dictionary.

Which and witch are homophones.

Live is the opposite of exist.

1, 2, 3!

Number the boxes 1, 2, or 3 to show the order of how things happened.

  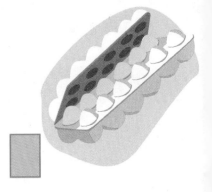

  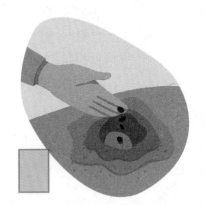

Now choose one of the stories and write a sentence telling what happened next.

_____

_____

Directing Traffic

Fill in the missing letter.

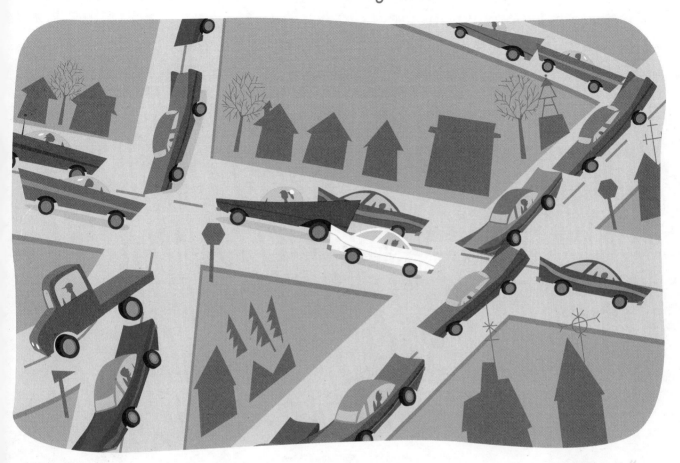

w __ r m   ___ o r d   ___ b o u t

re ___ d y   r e a d ___   c l e ___ n

c ___ r r y   c a r r ___   c l e a ___

___ a r m   c i t ___   a g a i ___

___ h i c h   ___ g a i n   o w ___

Now unscramble the letters to answer the question.
You will have to use one of the letters twice.

Which way did the cars go when the One Way signs were removed?

___ ___ ___   ___ ___ ___ ___

Taxi, Taxi

Get this taxi through the city streets and to the museum. Word pairs with correct synonyms are green lights. You can go right through. Word pairs that are not synonyms are red lights. You cannot pass through.

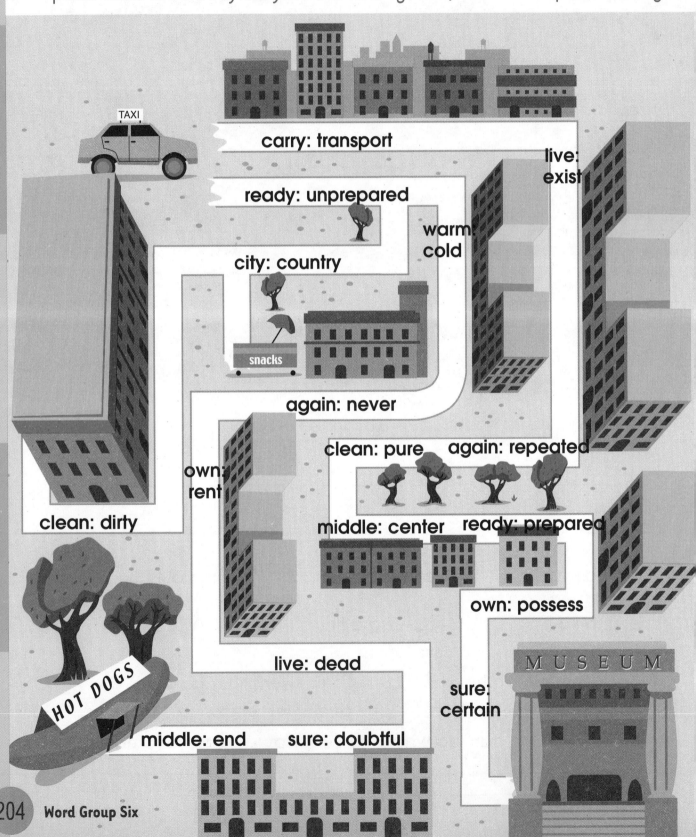

carry: transport

live: exist

ready: unprepared

warm: cold

city: country

snacks

again: never

clean: pure   again: repeated

own: rent

clean: dirty

middle: center   ready: prepared

own: possess

live: dead

HOT DOGS

MUSEUM

sure: certain

middle: end   sure: doubtful

Snail Mail

Put the words back into the letter in ABC order.

which   carry   about   though   word   clean

ready   own   middle   warm   again   sure   city

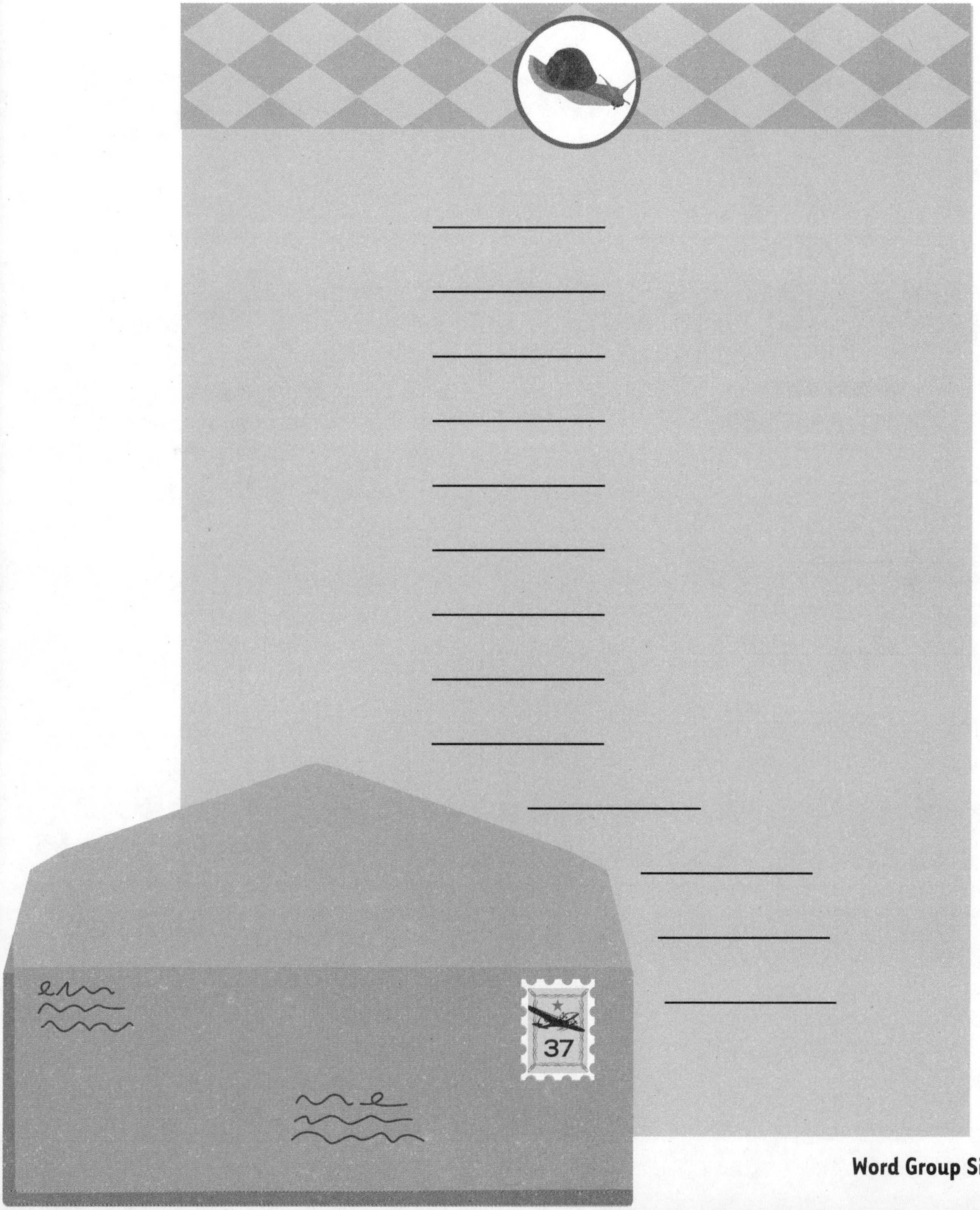

_____

_____

_____

_____

_____

_____

_____

_____

_____

_____

_____

Letter Blender

Use the letters in the blenders to make two words.

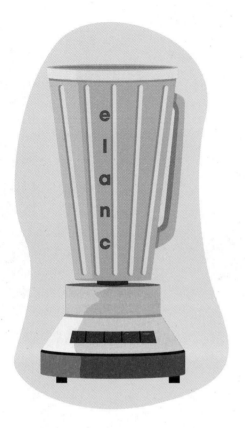

_____

_____

_____

_____

_____

_____

Keep the City Clean

Use words from the word box to finish the poem.
Hint: One word is used twice.

Word Box

about   carry   clean   ready   sure

I like my city neat and _____ .

I like its parks all fresh and green.

I don't mean to yell and shout,

but people shouldn't throw

    garbage _____ .

If I just leave it there to rot.

I'll _____ notice when it gets hot.

I can't wait another day.

Before I _____ it away.

My pup is always _____ to eat,

but I don't want him licking

what's on the street.

So, I'll pick it up. Yes, that's my plan

And carry it to a garbage can.

Now my street will be _____ for sure.

And I won't have to see garbage anymore.

I  The City

Can you read this letter from your friend in the city?
First, you'll have to figure out what the picture clues say and
write the words on the lines under the picture.

_____ live in the middle of the 🪑 + e _____ . H + _____

are a f + u _____ of m + 👁 _____ favorite things 2 _____ do

_____ the 🪑 + e _____ . I 💜 _____ 2 _____ play

_____ on my stoop. I 💜 _____ 2 _____ play ♟ _____

I 💜 _____ to eat warm _____ . I 💜 _____ 2 _____

walk across a bridge with my grandpa. I own a 🚲 _____ and I

💜 _____ to r + 👁 + d _____ ⚽ - b _____ around the

city, looking at the things. 📅 + 🐝 _____ u _____

🥫 _____ come 2 _____ visit me soon.

Opposite Land

Analogies are comparisons between two words. Complete these analogies using the words from the word box. The first one is done for you.

Hot is to cold as country is to ___city___.

Tall is to short as dirty is to _____ .

Sad is to happy as doubtful is to _____.

Now is to later as never is to _____.

Walk is to run as drop is to _____.

City Scramble

Unscramble the words on the subway cars
and write them on the lines.

_____

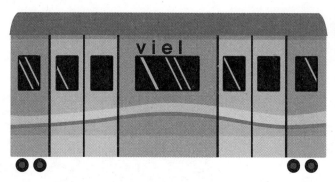

_____

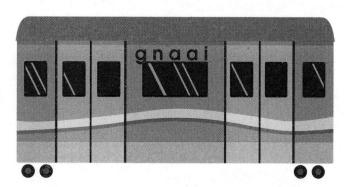

_____

_____

_____

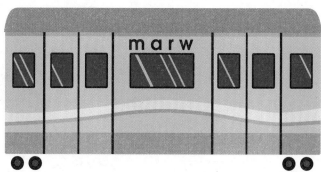

_____

Clean and Cleaned

Replace the orange words with words from the word box that mean the same thing but are in the present tense. You can use the same word more than once.

Word Box

clean   carry   own

This story is about how I **cleaned** _____ my room.

First I picked up every item I **owned** _____ and I

cleaned _____ them all off. Then I **carried**

_____ all my toys to the toy shelf. Last, I **carried**

_____ all my dirty clothes downstairs. Now that my

room is **cleaned**, _____ I could play in it all I

wanted. But I really don't want to mess anything up!

Ready to Race

Read the story. Number the sentences from 1 to 5 to show the order in which events happened.

The day of the big race had finally come. I had been practicing for months. Now the day of the race was finally here and I was sure that I was ready. I did some stretches to warm up my legs. I went out to the racetrack to line up. My spot was right in the middle. I took a deep breath of the warm air. I breathed deeply again. Now I just had to wait for the words. Then I heard them, "Get ready. Get set. Go." I was off! I shot down the middle of the race track like the wind. I didn't think about anything but the track under my feet and the finish line ahead. I made it to the finish line ahead of everyone else. I won! All that practice had paid off.

_____ She ran down the middle of the track.

_____ She won the race.

_____ She breathed the warm air.

_____ She stretched her legs to warm up.

_____ She practiced for months.

Climbing Ladders

Climb the ladders by filling in the missing word that shows how one word turns into another. The first one is done for you.

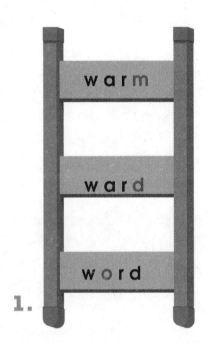

1.
- warm
- ward
- word

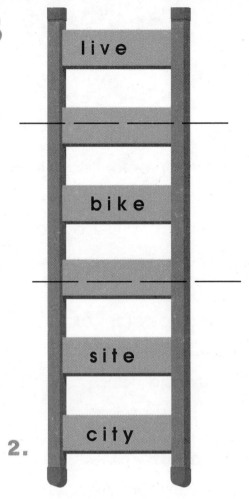

2.
- live
- _ _ _ _
- bike
- _ _ _ _
- site
- city

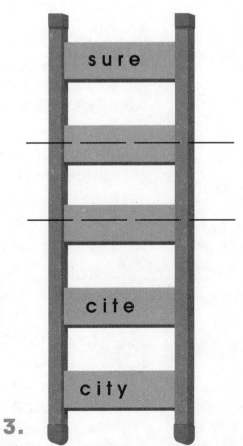

3.
- sure
- _ _ _ _
- _ _ _ _
- cite
- city

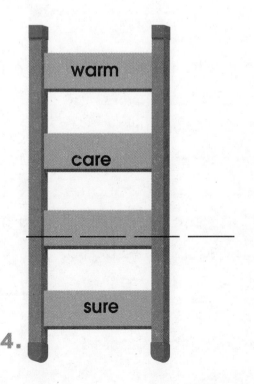

4.
- warm
- care
- _ _ _ _
- sure

Just Say the Word

You'll need

- a marker for each player (for example, a bean, a pebble, or a coin).
- a die
- a stopwatch (or wristwatch with a second hand)
- this game board

The Object of the Game

To be the first person to reach the WORD square.

How To Play

Each player begins at Start. Take turns rolling the die and moving that many squares. Follow the directions on the squares you land on. You have only 30 seconds to do so. If it takes you more than 30 seconds you have to move back as directed.

Say a word that rhymes with **though** and move ahead two squares. If you can't, move back one square.

Use the word **again** in a sentence and move ahead one square. If you can't, move back two squares.

Say a word that rhymes with **sure** and move ahead one square. If you can't, move back one square.

Say the opposite of **sure** and move ahead one square. If you can't, move back two squares.

Use the word **about** in a sentence and move ahead two squares. If you can't, move back one square.

Say a word that rhymes with **live** and move ahead two squares. If you can't, move back two squares.

Say something that you **carry** and move ahead one space. If you can't, move back one space.

Start

Say the opposite of **city** and move one square ahead. If you can't, move back one square.

Name one thing you could find in **city** and move head two quares. If you an't, move back ne square.

Say a word that rhymes with **word** and move ahead one space. If you can't, move back one space.

Say the opposite of **live** and move one square ahead. If you can't, move back one square.

Say a word that rhymes with **carry** and move ahead one square. If you can't, move back one square.

Say a word that means the same thing as **live** and move ahead two squares. If you can't, move back one square.

Say a word that means the opposite of **ready** and move ahead one square. If you can't, move back one square.

Use the word **which** in a sentence and move ahead two squares. If you can't, move back one square.

Say a word that rhymes with **own** and move ahead one square. If you can't, move back two squares.

Name an object that you might **clean** and move ahead two squares. If you can't, move back one square.

Use **word** in a sentence and move ahead two squares. If you can't, move back two squares.

Say a word that means that same thing as **ready** and move ahead one square. If you can't, move back two squares.

Say a synonym for **middle** and move ahead two squares. If you can't, move back one square.

Say the synonym of **carry** and move two squares ahead. If you can't, move back one square.

Say something that is **warm** and move ahead two squares. If you can't, move back two squares.

Use the word **though** in a sentence and move ahead two squares. If you can't, move back one square.

Say the opposite of **clean** and move ahead one space. If you can't, move back one square.

Word Group 6 Answer Key

183 1. about; 2. again; 3. carry; 4. city; 5. clean; 6. live; 7. middle; 8. own; 9. ready; 10. sure; 11. though; 12. warm; 13. which; 14. word; 7; 7

184 country; dirty; drop; cold; once

185 sure; warm; clean; middle; own; again

186–187 sure, clean; warm; own, again; middle; about, ready; The box numbers are: 3; 2; 5; 4; 1

188 marry/carry; pretty/city; teen/clean; bone/own; poor/sure; bow/though; storm/warm; pitch/which; bird/word

189 Nouns: city; word; **Adjectives:** clean; warm **Verbs:** carry; clean; live; warm

190 live; ready; warm; own; clean; see right

191 live; clean, carry; words; again

192 see right; 28

193 witch; which; which; witch

194 middle; word; warm; city

195 True; False; False; False; True; True; True

196 lime; rod; out; arm; hi; car

197 clean; warm; middle; own; sure

198 see right

199 answers will vary

200 Across: 2. again; 7. city; 8. though; 10. middle; 13. word; 14. clean **Down:** 1. ready; 3. about; 4. which; 5. warm; 6. sure; 9. carry; 11. live; 12. own

201 see right

202 Row 1: 3; 2; 1; Row 2: 1; 3; 2; Row 3: 3; 2; 1; answers will vary

203 column 1: a; a; a; w; w; **column 2:** w; y; y; y; **column 3:** a; a; n; n; n; any way

204 Follow maze through carry:transport; live:exist; again:repeated; clean/pure; middle/center; ready /prepared; own/possess; sure/certain

205 about; again; carry; city; clean; live; middle; own; ready; sure; though; warm; which; word

206 words may vary: clean/lance; live/evil/veil; own/now/won

207 clean; about; sure; carry; ready; clean

208 I; city; Here; few; my; to; in; city; love; to; ball; love; to; chess; love; pizza; love; to; bike; love; ride; all; Maybe; you; can; to

209 city; clean; sure; again; carry

210 column 1: carry; again; which; **column 2:** live; sure; warm

211 carry; live; sure; warm; which; again

212 4; 5; 3; 2; 1

213 2. live; like; bike; bite; site; city; 3. sure; cure; cute; cite; city; 4. warm; care; cure; sure

page 190
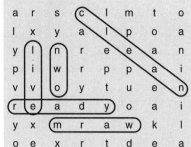
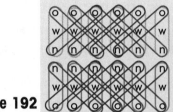

page 192
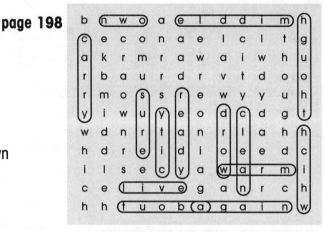

page 198
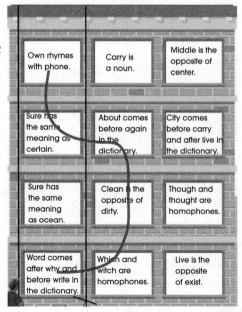

page 201

I Live in the City

In the city it is . . .

Lively and
Interesting
Very cool and so
Exciting.

In the city it is . . .
Nonstop.

Time to get up,
Hard to sleep,
Entertaining and always a

Celebration.
In the city it is . . .
Too much fun. So come visit.
You'll like it, too.

---

fold & assemble

City Beat

Written by Anne Schreiber
Illustrated by Greg Paprocki

Scholastic 100 Words Kids Need
to Read by 3rd Grade, Word Group 6

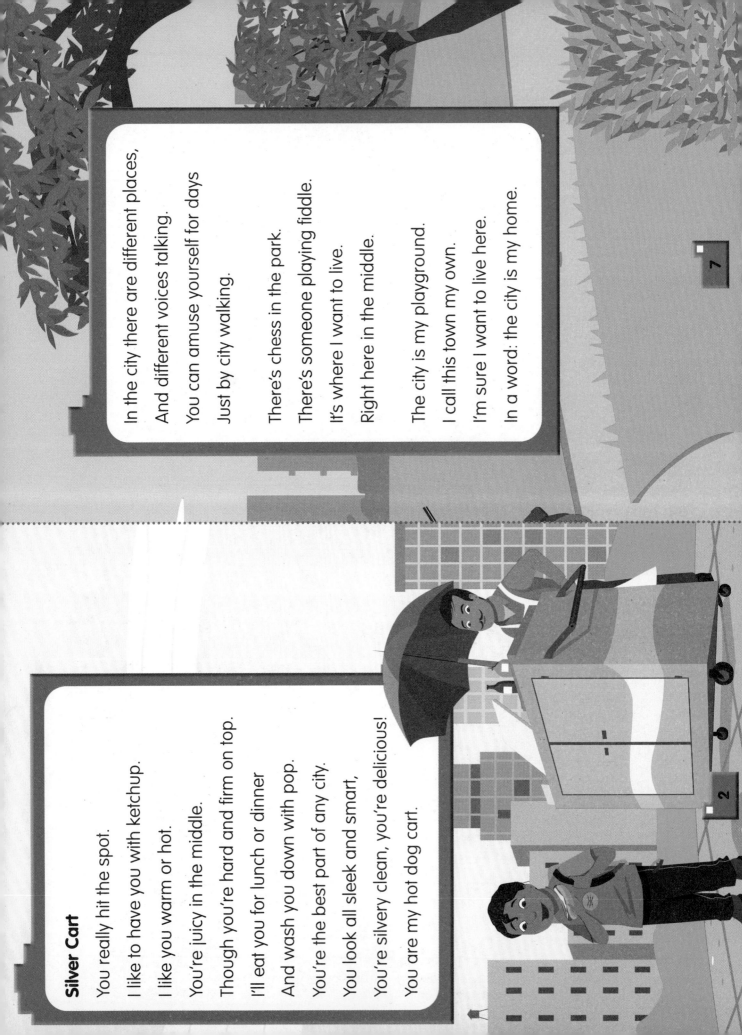

Silver Cart

You really hit the spot.
I like to have you with ketchup.
I like you warm or hot.
You're juicy in the middle.
Though you're hard and firm on top.
I'll eat you for lunch or dinner
And wash you down with pop.
You're the best part of any city.
You look all sleek and smart,
You're silvery clean, you're delicious!
You are my hot dog cart.

In the city there are different places,
And different voices talking.
You can amuse yourself for days
Just by city walking.

There's chess in the park.
There's someone playing fiddle.
It's where I want to live.
Right here in the middle.

The city is my playground.
I call this town my own.
I'm sure I want to live here.
In a word: the city is my home.

7

August Heat

Hot again in August.
Sprinklers in the park.
Cookouts in the yard.
Curtains fluttering through open windows.
Kids on the sidewalks
Whispering words
About fireflies and fans.
August in the city.
It's not just warm.
It's hot.
Hot again in August.

Haikus About the City

Sounds of the city.
Like being in the middle.
Of a kettle drum.

It's a warm spring day.
Someone is smiling at me.
Though I'm not sure why.

A million faces.
Pulling into the station.
Which way do I go?

Nothing bothers me.
I'm always sure and ready.
I'm from the city.

Carry me on your
cable car. Take me there and
take me back again.

Trouble with T's

Help Tracy fix her word list. Cross out the **t**'s that don't belong.
Add **t**'s to the words that need them.

beauiful	learnt	ogether
beween	neither	ttomorrow
differen	several	troublet
either	sraight	
frighen	today	yestertday

My Best Friend

Read the story. Then look in the word box to find the antonym for each word written in green. Write the antonyms on the lines.

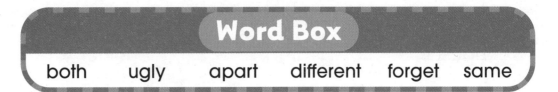

Word Box

both   ugly   apart   different   forget   same

My best friend and I do everything together.

We are very much alike.

We both love ice cream and neither of us like brussel sprouts.

We both love ice skating. We both hate mice.

We have a beautiful friendship.

I hope we are friends forever.

1. together _____

2. alike _____

3. neither _____

4. beautiful _____

Famous Words

Use the words in the word box to finish the famous sayings.
Hint: You may need to use capital letters.

Word Box

| straight | today | together | tomorrow | trouble | yesterday |

Birds of a feather flock _____.

Here today, gone _____.

_____ is the first day of the rest of your life.

A _____ arrow always hits the mark.

_____, all my _____ seemed
so far away.

A May Birthday

Read this poem. Find 8 words that rhyme with **today**. Write them in the tube.

In the month of May
We went away
To a water park
To swim and play.

Every day in the sun
We splashed and had a lot of fun.
We jumped in the pool
And slid down the slides
We went on wet and wild rides.

We ran through the spray
Of sprinklers and hoses
We got water in our ears

And water in our noses.
All in all I have to say
It was the absolute best way
To celebrate my birthday.

TODAY

Track It!

Making a chart can help you keep track of things.

Write 4 things under each heading
to show what you've done and what you have to do.
Hint: Include chores and fun things!

Yesterday	Today	Tomorrow
_____	_____	_____
_____	_____	_____
_____	_____	_____
_____	_____	_____

Family Fun

Use the words from the word box to complete the sentences.
Hint: You may need to use a capital letter.

Word Box

been	learn	neither	several	today	together

1. Have you _____ to a good movie this week?

2. I got _____ toys for my birthday.

3. I wonder what I will _____ in school today.

4. I have a music lesson _____ .

5. _____ my brother nor I like chocolate.

6. My family gets _____ to play games on Friday nights.

Simon the Superhero

Simon is a superhero who has lost one of his powers. Finish the sentences with words from the word box. Then follow the directions below to find out what superpower Simon has lost.

Word Box

yesterday	learn	been
tomorrow	trouble	today

1. Simon has __ __ __ __ a superhero for two days.
        ₁   ₂

2. Simon stills needs lessons to __ __ __ __ __ how to be a superhero.
                                       ₃

3. Simon got his superpowers __ __ __ __ __ __ __ __ __ .
                                 ₄   ₅

4. Simon lost one of his superpowers __ __ __ __ __.
                                          ₆

5. Simon needs to find this superpower before class

__ __ __ __ __ __ __ __.
   ₇

6. If Simon does not find his superpower, he will get into

__ __ __ __ __ __ __.
         ₈

Fill in the numbered letters in order to find out which superpower Simon lost.

__ __ __ __ __   __ __ __ __   __ __ __ __
8 6 5 2 3   1 2 6 7   2 4 2 5

Letter in a Bottle

Fill in the missing words to read the letter in a bottle.

Word Box

beautiful   different   frighten   several   together   trouble

To Whomever Finds this Letter,

I am on a _____ island. I have been here

for two straight months. At first, the animals here tried to

_____ me. Now they are my friends. There

are many _____ kinds of flowers here.

There are _____ kinds of fruit trees so I

have enough to eat. Yesterday I met some of the island

people and we are getting _____ for a

party tomorrow. Don't try to find me. I'm not in any

_____ and I love it here. I think I'll stay.

Suffix Slip-up

Whoops! The suffixes (word endings) in this report are mixed up. Look at the words in blue. Rewrite the correct word, using a suffix from the box.

Suffix Box

-ed	-ied	-ed
-ent	-ful	-ing
-ed		

For our science project we studying caterpillars for several days. We kept them in a special butterfly box. On the third day, we watching as they spun cocoons. Then they turns into butterflies. It was a beautifying thing to see. The butterflies were all differly colors. From this project, we learnful a lot about the life cycle of a butterfly. Tomorow we are goed to set our butterflies free.

_____   _____   _____

_____   _____   _____

_____

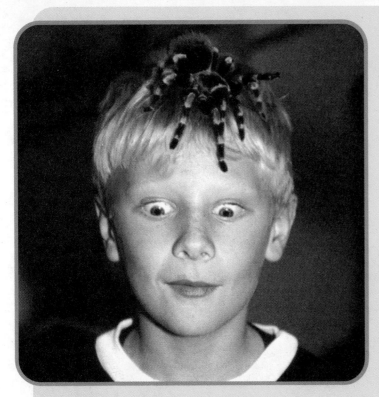

A Crazy Day at School

Use words from the word box to complete the story.

Word Box

beautiful	frighten	Several
been	Neither	together
different	straight	trouble

It has _____ a crazy day at school. We

had a _____ teacher today.

_____ of the kids at our table screamed.

A boy at our table got in a lot of _____.

I'll tell you what happened. The boy dropped a spider at

our table. I thought the spider was _____.

_____ my friend nor I were scared. We

went _____ to the new teacher.

The boy was just trying to _____ us.

My best friend and I were sitting _____

when all of this happened. It's always easier not being

scared when your best friend is sitting right next to you.

Bubble Surprise

Five words in each group are synonyms.
One word in each group is an antonym.
Put an X on each antonym.

concern

difficulty

ease

worry

trouble

problem

alarm

scare

terrify

upset

frighten

soothe

Name That Day

Complete the each sentence using **yesterday**, **today**, or **tomorrow**.

It was a beautiful afternoon. My mother asked, "What do you want to

do _____?" I told her I wanted to go the park. But my

sister wanted to go to the movies.

"It's so nice out _____, " my mother said. "I have

an idea. Let's go to the park _____ and we will go

the movies _____."

"I can't wait until _____," my sister said. The movie is

opening _____ and I want to be the first one in my class

to see it. Also, we went to the park just _____, remember?"

My mother said that even though we had gone to the park

_____, it was so beautiful outside _____

that this was definitely a day for the park.

"Besides," she told my sister, "_____ is another day."

Rhyme Time

Circle the words that rhyme with **straight**.

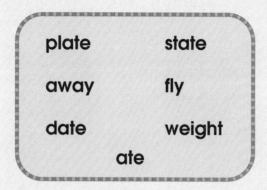

plate	state
away	fly
date	weight
	ate

Now finish this sentence using some
of the words you circled.

On a play _____ my friend and

I _____ a _____

full of apples and cheese.

Dunk It!

Get the ball in the basket by circling the ball with the opposite meaning of the word on the basket.

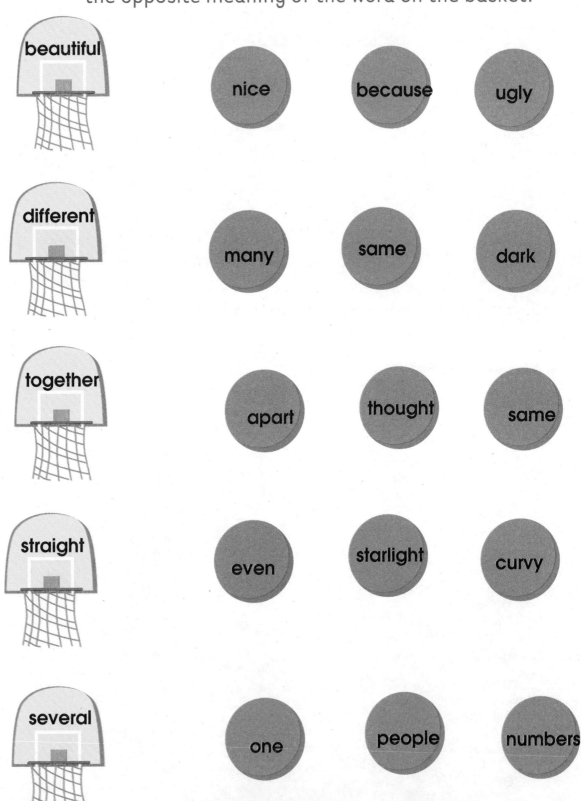

beautiful — nice — because — ugly

different — many — same — dark

together — apart — thought — same

straight — even — starlight — curvy

several — one — people — numbers

Mouse Mess

Unscramble the words in blue and write them on the lines. Then read this rhyming poem.

The trouble started sedrteyya   _____

When I went out to play.

I was lrveesa streets from my house   _____

When I saw a giant mouse.

I screamed. I ran

gtsiraht for my house.   _____

But this was no ordinary mouse.

He did not try to ihrtnefg me.   _____

Instead he asked me in for tea.

I chatted with him and his wife.

He wanted to ernal about my life.   _____

He asked me if I'd like to stay.

But I knew it was time to go away.

I wonder who'll I'll meet dytao.   _____

Uh-Oh!

Write a story that tells about the picture. Use the words **frighten**, **neither**, **together**, and **trouble** in your sentences.

_____

_____

_____

_____

_____

_____

_____

_____

Either or Neither

Use **either** or **neither** to finish the sentences.
Hint: You may need to use capital letters.

1. I don't like _____ of these hats.

either/neither

2. _____ of these coats fits me.

either/neither

3. _____ of these

either/neither

sweaters fits _____ of us.

either/neither

4. I think Lucy will like _____ of

either/neither

these necklaces.

5. _____ of these dogs bites.

either/neither

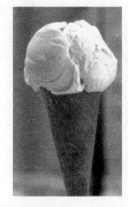

6. You can have _____

either/neither

vanilla or chocolate ice cream.

Weather Report

Read the weather report. Then answer the questions by filling in the bubbles.

Today has been a beautiful day so far. It looks as if the weather will be even nicer than it was yesterday. The sun is shining and the birds are chirping. Temperatures will soar to the high 90's.

Go outside and enjoy that sun while you can. There is a storm on the way. Tomorrow will start out dark and cloudy. Then it will become wet and cold. It will rain all day. It will rain all week. It might even snow.

1. Which word means the same as **singing** in this story?
- ○ a. shining
- ○ b. soar
- ○ c. chirping

2. Why does the weather report tell you to go outside and enjoy the sun while you can?
- ○ a. Tomorrow it will rain.
- ○ b. The rain will help the drought.
- ○ c. It is nighttime.

3. Which words in this report have the same meaning as **coming**?
- ○ a. on the way
- ○ b. will become
- ○ c. will start out

4. In the dictionary, the word **beautiful** appears
- ○ a. after the word bouncy
- ○ b. between apples and cars
- ○ c. before the word band

5. Which word means the same as **soar**?
- ○ a. run
- ○ b. rise
- ○ c. ripe

My Friend from Jupiter

Fill in the words before
you read the story.
Then read it out loud
for a laugh!

When you first meet my friend

_____ he might frighten you.
　　name

He isn't from around here and he looks

it. He's from another planet. On his

planet, they think he is beautiful. But

here on earth, people think he's

_____. He has long
　　adjective

_____ hair and several
　　color

_____ in the middle of his head.
　plural noun

He has the body of a _____
　　　　　　　　　　　animal

When he talks, his voice is high and

_____. He sometimes spits when
　adjective

he talks. But once you get to know my

friend, you will really like him. He's been

a good friend to me.

　Even if he does look like a

_____ .
　vegetable

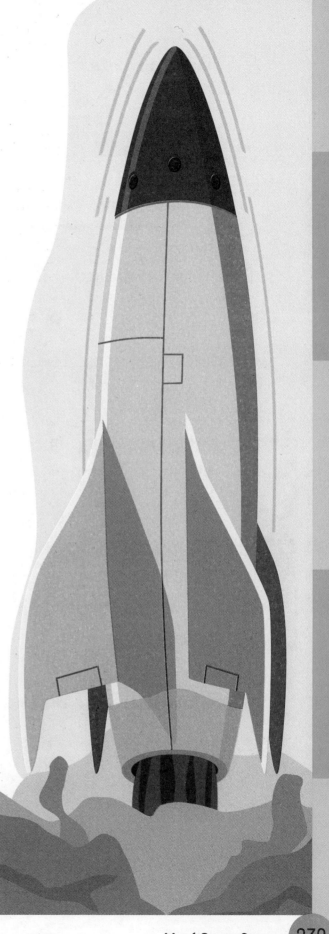

My Week at Grandma's

Use the words from the word box to finish the letter below.
Hint: You may need to use capital letters.

Word Box

different	frighten	today	straight,	neither
yesterday	beautiful	tomorrow	together	

Dear Mom and Dad,

I am having the best week at Grandma's. Every day we have

done something _____. Every day has been better than the

one before. _____ we went swimming with the dolphins.

Grandma said she thought the dolphins would

_____ her, but when she saw how

_____ they were she wasn't scared at

all. We touched them and swam with them.

_____ of us wanted to get out of the

water. It was great. _____ we went to

an amusement park and had hot dogs and ice cream for lunch. It is

supposed to be sunny out _____, so we are going

_____ to the beach. I have to go now. Grandma and I are

going to the movies _____ .

Love,

Me

Alphabet Soup

Write the missing letters on the lines below.

t __ day   di __ __ erent

tr __ __ uble   __ righten

t __ m __ rr __ w   beautl __ ul

Missing Letter ___   Missing Letter ___

severa __   lea __ n

__ earn   neithe __ __

troub __ e   st __ aight

Missing Letter ___   Missing Letter ___

__ oge __ her   d __ fferent

yes __ erday   e __ ther

frigh __ en   stra __ ght

Missing Letter ___   Missing Letter ___

Juggling

The letters in these balls spell **together**. Juggle the letters around until you spell the words missing in the following sentences.

1. I gave the birthday girl _____ present.

2. "_____ away from me!" I yelled at the bully.

3. I went to the market _____ buy some bread.

4. _____ once was an ugly duckling.

5. On the farm there was a _____.

6. "We're over _____ !" I called.

7. "Ouch!" I stubbed my little _____.

8. My best friend and I do everything _____.

Casey Can't Catch

Casey can't catch vowels. Help him out.
Use the vowels he dropped to correctly
spell the words below.

t m r r w _____

b t f l _____

f r g h t n _____

s v r l _____

s t r g h t _____

d f f r n t _____

Pizza Party

A class voted on when to have a pizza party. This graph shows the results of the vote.

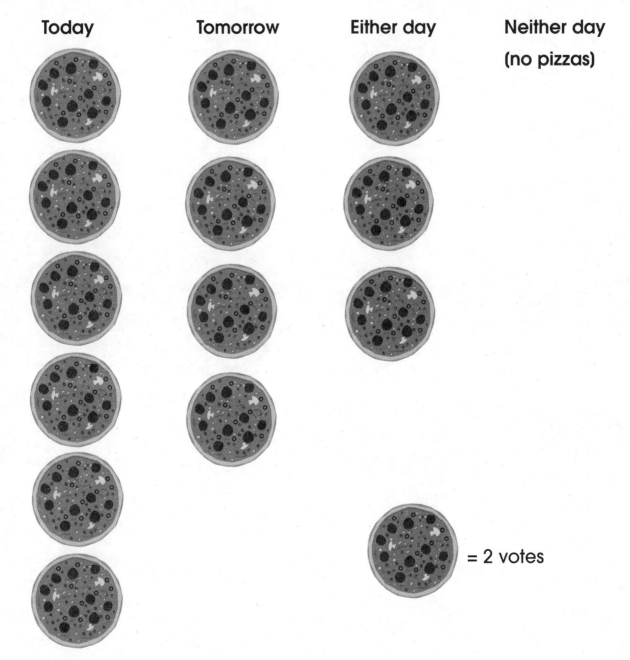

Today	Tomorrow	Either day	Neither day (no pizzas)

= 2 votes

1. How many children voted to have the pizza party today? _____

2. How many children voted to have the pizza party tomorrow? _____

3. How many children voted to have the pizza party either day? _____

4. How many children don't want the pizza party today or tomorrow? _____

beautiful	been	different
frighten	learn	neither
several	straight	together
trouble	either	Wild Card

Stuck in Space, see page 249

Word Card   Word Card   Word Card

Word Card   Word Card   Word Card

Word Card   Word Card   Word Card

Word Card   Word Card   Word Card

Stuck in Space, see page 249

Aliens Attack!
Escape to
yesterday.

Black Hole.
Move back 3
spaces.

Time Warp
Takes you back
2 yesterdays

Friendly Creature
Helps you move
2 spaces toward
tomorrow.

Stormy Night.
Stay where you are
for one turn.

Stop to refuel.
Lose a turn.

Catch a ride on
a comet.
Move forward
one space.

Beam aboard a
traveler.
Take him back
to yesterday.

Lost in space.
Go back to today.

Ride a roller coaster
in space.
Move to the next
pick a card.

Meteor shower!
Go back
three spaces.

Lost track of time.
Go back to today.

Stuck in Space, see page 249

Time
Travel
Card

Time
Travel
Card

Time
Travel
Card

Time
Travel
Card

Time
Travel
Card

Time
Travel
Card

Time
Travel
Card

Time
Travel
Card

Time
Travel
Card

Time
Travel
Card

Time
Travel
Card

Time
Travel
Card

Stuck in Space, see page 249

Stuck in Space

You'll Need

- 12 Word cards (page 245)
- 12 Time Travel cards (page 247)
- game board (pages 250–251)
- a game piece for each player (coin, button, bean, etc.)
- a die

How To Play

1. Cut out all the Word cards and Time Travel cards. Place them face down in separate piles.
2. Open to the gameboard. Put your game pieces at the beginning, near TODAY.
3. Roll the die. Move your game piece the number of dots on the die.

   - If you land on Yesterday, stay there and do nothing.
   - If you land on Pick a Time Travel Card, pick a card. Follow the directions on the card.
   - If you land on Pick a Word Card, pick a card and follow the directions on the game board using the word on your word card.
   - If you pick the wild card, another player gets to give you a word.

4. The first person to reach TOMORROW wins.

Today

Pick a Word card. Say the opposite of the word.

Yesterday

Pick a Time Travel card.

Pick a Word card. Say the word. Then close your eyes and spell the word.

Yesterday

Yesterday

Pick a Word card. Use the word in a sentence about space.

Pick a Time Travel card.

Pick a Time Travel card.

Pick a Word card. Use the word to describe an alien.

Yesterday

Pick a Word card. Say a word that means the same.

Pick a Time Travel card.

Pick a Word card. Say the word 10 times fast.

Pick a Word card. Use the word to describe another player.

Pick a Word card. Make up a poem with the word.

Yesterday

Pick a Word card. Say the word in a sentence that is a question.

Yesterday.

Pick a Time Travel card.

Pick a Time Travel card.

Pick a Time Travel card.

Pick a Word card. Say the past tense of the word.

Pick a Word card. Say a word that rhymes.

Tomorrow

Word Group 7 Answer Key

221 add t's: beautiful; between; different; frighten; straight; together;
cross out t's: learn; tomorrow; trouble; yesterday;
correct as is: either; neither; several; today

222 1. apart; 2. different; 3. both; 4. ugly

223 together; tomorrow; Today; straight; Yesterday; troubles

224 May: away; play; day; spray; say; way; birthday

225 answers will vary

226 1. been; 2. several; 3. learn; 4. today; 5. Neither; 6. together

227 1. been; 2. learn; 3. yesterday; 4. today; 5. tomorrow; 6. trouble; laser beam eyes

228 beautiful; frighten; different; several; together; trouble

229 studied; watched; turned; beautiful; differently; learned; going

230 been; different; several; trouble; beautiful; Neither; straight; frighten; together

231 put an X on ease; soothe

232 today; today; today; tomorrow; tomorrow; today; yesterday; yesterday; today; tomorrow

233 circle: plate; date; ate; state; weight write: date; ate; plate

234 circle: ugly; same; apart; curvy; one

235 yesterday; several; straight; frighten; learn; today

236 answers will vary

237 1. either; 2. Neither; 3. Neither, either; 4. either; 5. Neither; 6. either

238 1c; 2a; 3a; 4. b; 5b

239 answers will vary

240 different; Yesterday; frighten;, beautiful; Neither; Today;
tomorrow; straight; together

241 o; l; t; f; r; i

242 1. her; 2. Get; 3. to; 4. There; 5. hog; 6. here; 7. toe; 8. together

243 tomorrow; beautiful; frighten; several; straight; different

244 1. 12; 2. 8; 3. 6; 4. 0

The king raced up to the royal chef. "Didn't I just tell you yesterday about ringing that bell too loudly?" the king started to say. Then he saw the princess and the new nanny laughing and dancing together.

"It's been so long since I've seen her this happy," the king cried. Then he turned to the royal chef and said, "Maybe tomorrow you can ring the bell even louder."

8

fold & assemble

Princess Scaredy-Cat

Written by Kathryn McKeon
Illustrated by Jackie Snider

Scholastic *100 Words Kids Need to Read by 3rd Grade*, Word Group 7

1

Soon it was time for dinner. The royal chef rang the dinner bell. CLANG! The princess jumped straight into the air and covered her ears.

"Oh, what a fun dinner dance," said the new nanny. She jumped straight into the air and waved her arms around. The princess stared at the new nanny and laughed. This nanny sure was different.

Once there was a beautiful princess who was afraid of everything.

"Don't ring the dinner bell too loud," the King told the royal chef. "It will frighten the princess."

"Please keep the horses several yards away from the castle," the Queen told the royal stable boy. "They will frighten the princess."

Next the pair headed off together to the royal playground.

"Slide or swings?" said the new nanny.

"I have not been on either one," said the princess.

"They frighten me."

"Today will be different," said the new nanny. "You will learn how to swing."

The princess sat down on the swing. After a few tries she began to smile—and swing!

The royal nanny had been with the princess since she was born. But it was getting hard to keep straight all the different things that would frighten the princess.

"That kid is a ton of trouble," the royal nanny said. "Today is my last day." Neither the king nor the queen blinked.

"No problem," said the king. "We will just get a new nanny tomorrow."

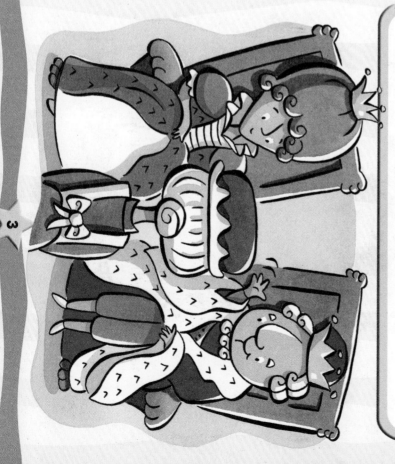

The new nanny took the princess straight to the barn. The princess stood several feet away from the horses.

"Aren't they beautiful?" the new nanny said, pointing at two black ponies.

"They frighten me," said the princess. The new nanny gave the princess several apples to feed the ponies. "That tickles," giggled the princess.

The next day the new nanny arrived. "Yesterday we had a little trouble," the queen explained to the princess. "Today you have a new nanny."

The new nanny was very different. When the king told her about all the things that frightened the princess, the new nanny just laughed. "She will learn," the new nanny said.